BYZANTINE PAINTING

The Last Phase

DAVID TALBOT RICE

BYZANTINE PAINTING

The Last Phase

THE DIAL PRESS, INC. NEW YORK, 1968

Originally published in England under the same title
by George Weidenfeld & Nicolson Limited

Copyright © 1968 by David Talbot Rice

Library of Congress Catalog Card Number: 68-28689

Manufactured in Germany

Contents

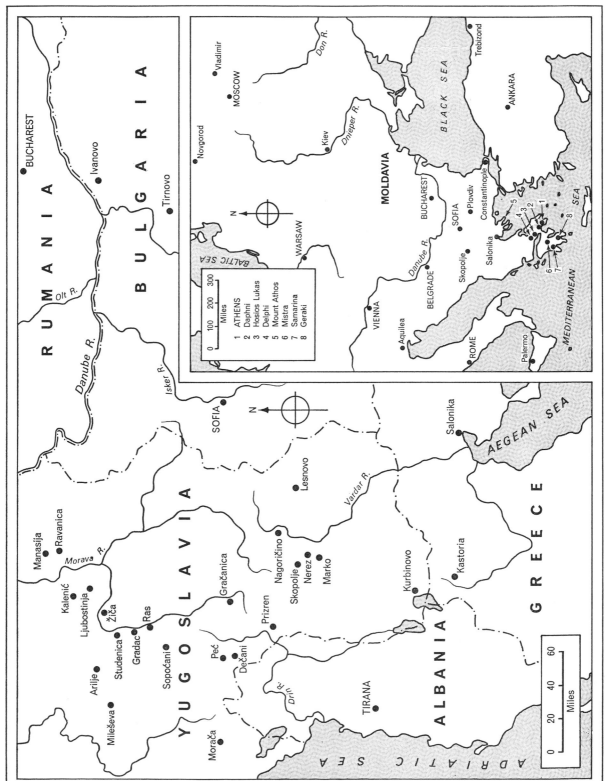

The most important centres of Byzantine painting during its last phase.

Preface

Had Robert Byron not gone down with a vessel which was torpedoed in the Mediterranean in 1940, this book might well have been one of joint authorship, like that which we wrote together in 1930, *The Birth of Western Painting*, in which we sought to draw more general attention to the interest of later Byzantine art and to the role played by Byzantium as a source of much that was subsequently done in the west. At that time the quality of later Byzantine art was far from generally recognised, and our book was written as an apologia, in the spirit of a crusade. Since then nearly forty years have passed. They have been years during which a very great deal of new material has been discovered and throughout which study has advanced by leaps and bounds, and today there are few who would seek to deny the quality of later Byzantine art, still less the importance of the role that Byzantium has played as a source of inspiration in the west. Yet, though ease of travel has made some of the monuments more readily familiar, many are still not very easy of access, and though good colour plates have become numerous, the basic publications in which many of the monuments are considered have been made in journals or in languages not normally available to the average reader in Western Europe and in America, and in the east of Europe, where art of this family is familiar, frontier and currency restrictions have made comparative study wellnigh impossible. There thus seemed room for a book which would bring all the material together in the compass of a single volume, fully illustrated with plates of high quality, and it is with the object of filling a gap which is as obvious to the east of the Iron Curtain as it is in the west that this book is offered to the public.

It should thus be regarded primarily as a guide in a somewhat unfamiliar field; for a fuller treatment of the basic material the reader must turn to the basic publications of such scholars as Radojčić or Djurić in Serbo-Croat, of Miatev or Mavrodinov in Bulgarian, of Lazarev in Russian, or of P. A. Underwood on Kariye Camii in English. But the writer has devoted many years to the study of Byzantine art as a whole, and to the last phase, between the conquest of Constantinople by the Latins in 1204 and the Turks in 1453, in particular, and the book contains also many of his own views and conclusions. Some of these are essentially personal, and other scholars may wish to dispute them; some may be proved right or wrong by discoveries of new monuments in the future, for the field is far from exhausted; but others, more especially those relating to the value of later Byzantine art, using the word in its widest sense, will, it is hoped, be generally accepted.

The book first saw the light in the form of a series of lectures delivered under the auspices of the Ferens Foundation in the University of Hull; they were prepared while the author enjoyed a Visiting Fellowship at the British School of Archaeology in Athens in the spring of 1964. But since then the lectures have been considerably revised and new material has been added, in order to make the text suitable for publication in book form. And though it was of course possible to illustrate the lectures more lavishly with slides than can be done here with plates, it is hoped that the illustrations to this book will not only make a great deal of little-known material more generally familiar, but will also serve to show the very high and lively quality of much of this later Byzantine painting.

The book is in the first place offered as a homage to the memory of Gabriel Millet, with whom I learnt and whose arduous and painstaking journeys at the end of the last century and in the earlier years of this not only set an example to and furnished a model for all workers in the field, but also made it possible for scholars to pursue their work at home, a task which would otherwise have been impossible. And in the second place it is offered to my wife, in whose company I have visited nearly all the monuments mentioned here, and whose help and comments through many years have immeasurably assisted what I have done and stimulated work which might otherwise never have been undertaken; and finally it is dedicated to all those scholars in various countries who have so warmly welcomed my wife and myself on numerous visits. I should like to take this opportunity of expressing my thanks to the Managing Committee of the British School at Athens for appointing me as Visiting Fellow in 1964 and to the officers of the school for their friendly welcome. I should like to thank also all those others who have directly or indirectly helped in the preparation of this book, more especially those individuals who have furnished me with photographs over a long period of time and those official bodies which have allowed me to make use of material in their care. Under the first head I would like particularly to mention Madame Sotiriou, Professor Xyngopoulos and Monsieur Chatzidakis in Greece, Professor Radojćić, Professor Ljubinković and Mr Milković-Pepek in Yugoslavia, Professor V. N. Lazarev and Madame Alice Bank in the USSR and Mr Ralph Hoddinott in Britain. And under the second I am especially indebted to the Walters Art Gallery at Baltimore, the Dumbarton Oaks Research Institute and the National Gallery at Washington in the USA, to the Vatican Library in Italy, to the Byzantine Museum in Athens, and to the Departments for the Conservation of Ancient Monuments in Serbia and Macedonia. And finally I am indebted to Mr Ghasilov in the USSR and to Miss Josephine Powell in Rome for a number of photographs specially taken for this volume.

D. Talbot Rice

1

The Twelfth-Century Renaissance in Byzantine Art

From the point of view of political history the age between 1056, when the Great Macedonian dynasty came to an end, and 1204, when Constantinople fell to the Venetian and Latin adventurers of the Fourth Crusade, was, to say the least, depressing. In 1071 the Byzantine army was defeated by the Seljuks at Manzikert and within a few years the whole of upland Asia Minor was in Moslem hands; Byzantine power in southern Italy was gradually diminishing; throughout the twelfth century the Southern Slavs were asserting themselves and establishing control over what is today Serbia and northern Macedonia; by 1185 Basil II's victories over the Bulgars had been avenged and the northern Balkans had become independent. And, as the frontiers of the Byzantine Empire were withdrawn, so affairs at home took on a gradually worsening complexion; the peasantry was impoverished and unjustly taxed; there was lack of employment in the country, there was universal poverty, bribery and extortion were rife, and the administration corrupt. At best the emperors were unable to arrest the decay, at worst they were ready to exploit the situation to their own advantage. Yet, despite all the outward signs of decline, life in aristocratic circles continued with but little change; the nobles were rich and prosperous, imperial expenditure was lavish, and the ceremonial pomp of the court was to all intents hardly affected. Expenditure on the endless imperial functions continued without abatement; the love of ostentation was if anything greater than before; the emperors were still ready to squander vast sums on ephemeral entertainments or to sponsor artistic activities on a scale little less lavish than that which had pertained in the days when the empire extended from Persia to Italy, or when the wealth and prosperity of the empire aroused amazement and envy throughout the world.

Yet, even if the frontiers were limited, the internal situation perilous, and the state impoverished, the repute of Byzantine culture overseas was, so far as we can judge, in no way diminished; rulers in Russia and the Balkans, in Venice and in Sicily, still turned to Byzantium as the world's most progressive centre of thought and art, just as they had done when Byzantine imperial power was at its apex, and Byzantine craftsmen were still employed in virtually every corner of the civilised world; only in this way can we explain the mosaics of Kiev, of Venice and of Sicily, the wall paintings of the Balkans, of Russia and of Cyprus, the illuminations of Georgian manuscripts, or even the paintings done for the Latin rulers of Jerusalem; none of these things could have been produced without the assistance of Byzantine craftsmen, and none could have been conceived but for the skills and traditions that had been accumulated over the centuries in the Byzantine capital. Yet today we know but little of what was actually done in Constantinople. As is alas only too often the case with Byzantine art, we have to complete the picture of what once existed from very incomplete data; so much has perished, so much has been destroyed. But the surviving monuments, when carefully and painstakingly interrogated, can tell us an interesting and a surprisingly clear story, even though most of them are on the periphery; and few though they are, they still furnish enough evidence to enable us to classify the art of the later eleventh and earlier twelfth centuries into a series of distinct categories. It was from a blend of all of them that was developed the progressive style which we term the style of the *Revival*. The story of its development will be our main concern in the pages that follow. At the outset each of these categories may be briefly described.

The first may be termed the Conservative style; it is best represented by the major part of the mosaic decoration of the Church of Daphni near Athens in Greece[1]. There the compositions are impressive, the figures are well modelled, and the treatment is essentially classical, so that at times the paintings make one think of the sculptures of ancient Greece (Plate 1). These mosaics are rich, elegant, beautiful, and represent what was perhaps the culmination of the monumental style of mid-Byzantine art. They may be contrasted with other work of the age, where a more linear style was to the fore, as for example in the mosaic in Hagia Sophia at Constantinople known as the *John Panel*, which dates from 1118 (Plate 5), and where the work is rather dry and hard, though none the less elegant. The same manner is to be found in ivories and miniatures of the age and distinguishes them from the more robust ones of the tenth century. Distinct again are certain other works where an almost exaggerated naturalism, and a certain heaviness of treatment were to the fore, as we can see, for example, in sculptures like one in marble on a fairly large scale, representing the Virgin, which is now in the Museum of Antiquities at Istanbul, or one of smaller proportions in green porphyry, now in the Victoria and Albert Museum; it bears the name of the Emperor Nicephorus Botiniates (1078–1081)[2]. To such works as these we may assign the designation of the Personal Style, for they are intimate and individual. Finally we may distinguish what may be termed the Expressive style, of which the great *Pantocrator* at the summit of the dome at Daphni is the most striking example (Plate 3); it is certainly the most awe-inspiring and also probably the most powerful rendering of Christ the Almighty ever conceived in Christian art and stands out as a work of quite astonishing brilliance and daring.

Of these various styles the most widespread and important around 1100 was probably that which was to the fore in the mosaics of Daphni, which we have termed the Conservative. Its ideals are clearly to be seen in the scene of the *Crucifixion* (Plate 1). No emotion is permitted to enter into the interpretation. The Virgin, tall and austere, points to the figure of our Lord as symbol of the faith; there is no hint of motherly affection, no intimacy. St John attests the event with a gesture, but no more; our Lord's body is firm and erect; there are no signs of the agony of the cross, no human weakness, no suffering or sorrow obtrude themselves; even Christ's eyes are open as in life. In fact, the mosaic is wholly a symbol. A similar approach characterises the scene of the *Nativity* in the south-east pendentive of the dome (Plate 2). The Virgin, formal and restrained, sits upright, a goddess rather than a mother who has just given birth; there is grandeur but no intimacy, no tenderness. A similar restraint characterises the other scenes. Subsidiary matter, trees, buildings, supporting figures, are reduced to the minimum necessary to illustrate the text, and there is little attempt to convey depth or recession (Plate 4). Equally significant is the way the figures are conceived and the costumes modelled, for they are all impressive, sculpturesque; their character is best described as neo-Attic.

If the word Renaissance were to be interpreted as denoting no more than a return to the past, the Daphni mosaics would undoubtedly warrant the application of the term. But that would be to use the word in far too narrow a sense; it must surely imply also the idea of a revival in spirit, a recreation of life, movement and emotion in art as well as that of a return to past excellence; for that we must look not so much to Daphni and to work done at the very end of the eleventh century, but rather to the second quarter of the twelfth, when the evidence suggests that a new style was being born. It is exemplified for us in the lovely icon known as *Our Lady of Vladimir*, now in the Tretyakov Gallery at Moscow (Plate I). Here a wholly new spirit dominates art. The pose which is designated as the Virgin of Tenderness (*Eleousa* in Greek or *Umilenye* in Russian) is one that is essentially humanist, personal and intimate; the Child's cheek is pressed against the Virgin's in love, his arm passes round her neck in affection; the expressions are gentle, and the composition is essentially that of adoring mother and loving child; the conception is far removed from that of the earlier iconographical type, the Indicator of the Way (*Hodegetria*), where the Virgin simply points to the child as basis of the Faith. In fact the interpretation of the concept of love has become the aim of art, rather than the mere depiction of the two figures as symbols of divinity.

The history of this panel is well attested in the texts. It was, it would seem, painted in Constantinople between 1125 and 1130, to the order of a Russian patron. Thence it was taken to Kiev, then to Vyshegorod, then in 1185 to Vladimir, and finally to Moscow. Its cleaning in 1918 disclosed the fact that only the two faces are original; the rest has been repainted. One authority, Konrad Onasch, has even suggested that the original icon was destroyed when the Tartars looted Vladimir in 1237, and that the painting we have is a copy done in Russia at that time[3]. There is little evidence to support this theory, but even if Dr Onasch is correct, the rules governing the reproduction of icons were so strict that the pose of the figures, the tender expressions and the humanistic approach would undoubtedly have pertained to the original twelfth-century work and not only to the copy. And though it cannot be claimed that the Virgin of Vladimir is the earliest example of the *Eleousa* type that we know, for it was already in existence in Egypt several centuries before[4], the earlier versions are rigid and severe; it was only in the twelfth century that the humanistic traits began to be stressed and it was not till the end of the century that the iconographic type of 'Our Lady of Tenderness' became at all universal.

It is interesting to contrast this intimate and profoundly expressive painting with the mosaic known as the *John Panel* in Hagia Sophia at Constantinople, which is only very slightly earlier in date; it was set up in 1118 and depicts the Emperor John Comnenos and his Queen Irene with the Virgin and Child between them (Plate 5). Here the understanding and feeling are utterly different. The delineation is hard and dry, the style linear, there is no intimacy and the figures — especially that of the Virgin — are conventional and impersonal. If later Byzantine art has sometimes been condemned as severe and unsympathetic, we see here justification of that condemnation, notwithstanding the brilliance of the colour and grandeur of the composition. Nothing could be further removed — granting a marked degree of competence — from the intimate delicacy of the Vladimir Madonna. Yet an adjacent mosaic which depicts the Emperor's son Alexios, done some four years later than the main panel, is more personal and individual (Plate 7). It is indeed a very intimate and moving study, for the prince was sickly and died at an early age; the touch of death is already apparent in the mosaic portrait.

No very extensive passage of time can surely separate this mosaic and the painting *Our Lady of Vladimir* from the superb composition that faces the former across the eastern bay of the south gallery of Hagia Sophia, namely the great *Deesis* composition, where Christ is shown between the Virgin and St John the Baptist (Plates II and 6). The style is painterly, the work astonishingly delicate, even the effect of a green undercoat which characterised paintings of the age has been reproduced through the use of unusually small cubes. Both technically and aesthetically speaking this is a mosaic of outstanding quality; it is even safe to say that it is perhaps the finest of all the mosaics that have come down to us from the Byzantine world. And it is characterised by a profoundly humanistic outlook; the Virgin is tender, sweet and pensive; St John, generally a somewhat rugged figure, is kindly and sympathetic; Christ is loving, human, personal, yet at the same time majestic and truly divine. We see here Christ the 'Son of Man', even the 'Man of Sorrows', and it represents a wholly different conception from that of the awesome judge in the dome at Daphni.

Opinions have varied considerably with regard to the date of this mosaic. Whittemore, who was responsible for uncovering it and who first published it, assigned it to around 1130, basing his views partly on the epigraphy of the inscriptions that designate the figures, and partly on stylistic similarities that the mosaic shows to the icon *Our Lady of Vladimir*. Indeed, for a time Whittemore believed it to be of even earlier date and this view was also held by C. R. Morey, who considered the mosaic to be a work of the eleventh century, done before what he termed the decadence of the twelfth had set in — but he wrote without taking sufficiently into account the progress towards humanism that it shows or the very high quality of much of later Byzantine art. He was indeed still governed by the prejudice voiced by Peirce and Tyler that no good work was done in later years and that all Byzantine art of quality belonged to the Macedonian Renaissance[5]. Grabar favours a dating in the later part of the twelfth century, while Lazarev has written at some length in support of one before 1150, basing his arguments on what he terms the linear stylisation of the faces. He compares the Christ to one in the Palatine chapel at Palermo (*c.* 1145); the St John, he shows, is rendered in a manner close to the Christ at Cefalù (*c.* 1148) or the St Simeon at Nerez (*c.* 1164), while the Virgin may be compared to one on a twelfth-century icon in the monastery of St Catherine on Mount Sinai; he even notes the similarities with the figures standing on either side of the Crucifixion at Daphni (*c.* 1100), though the degree of humanism and tenderness is much more marked in the Hagia Sophia mosaic[6].

The contrary view, that the mosaic is to be dated after rather than before the Latin occupation of Constantinople (1204–61) has been upheld by Galassi, Bettini and Demus[7]. Bettini's proposal that the mosaic should be dated to the fifteenth century was surely dictated by a preconception that so humanistic a work must have been inspired from Italy, and can now be discarded even though it would have been in accord with the thesis of Ainalov, put forward in 1917, that the Palaeologan style developed as a result of contacts with the west following upon the crusading conquest of Constantinople in 1204[8]. The researches undertaken by Gabriel Millet in the Balkans early in this century and the work of other scholars had begun to sow doubts as to the validity of this thesis even before the First World War, and the discovery by Okunev in 1927 of wall paintings at Nerez near Skopolje in Yugoslavia, dated to 1164, but in a wholly new, lively and humanistic style, finally

2, 3, 4 Daphni, Attica. Mosaics; c. 1100 *(above)* the *Nativity*; *(below left)* the *Pantocrator* in the dome; *(below right) Joachim and the Angel.*

5   Hagia Sophia, Constantinople. Mosaic; the *John Panel*; c. 1118.

6   *(below)* Hagia Sophia, Constantinople. Mosaic; the *Deesis*; mid-twelfth century.

8, 9 Nerez, Macedonia. Wall paintings;
c. 1164; *(above)* the *Transfiguration*;
(left) a *saint*.

7 *(opposite)* Hagia Sophia, Constantinople.
Mosaic portrait of *Alexius Comnenos*;
c. 1122.

12 *(above)* Kurbinovo, Macedonia. Wall painting; the *Transfiguration*; 1191.

10 *(opposite above)* Nerez, Macedonia. Wall painting; the *Deposition*; 1164.

11 *(opposite below)* Nerez, Macedonia. Wall painting; the *Lamentation*; 1164.

13 Nerez, Macedonia. Wall painting; the *Nativity of the Virgin – Washing of the child*; 1164

14 Nerez, Macedonia. Wall painting; the *Nativity of the Virgin – a servant*; 1164.

20

16 Kurbinovo, Macedonia. Wall painting; *St Panteleimon*; 1191.

15 Nerez, Macedonia. Wall painting; *St Panteleimon*; 1164.

17, 18, 19 Kurbinovo, Macedonia. Wall paintings; c. 1191. *(opposite)* The *Angel of the Annunciation*; *(above right)* the *Prophetess Anna*; *(below right)* detail of the *Lamentation*.

21 *(above)* The Cathedral of Monreale, Sicily. Mosaic; *The Construction of the Ark*; end of the twelfth century.

20 *(opposite)* The Martorana, Palermo, Sicily. Mosaic; the *Presentation*; c. 1151.

23 *(below right)* Samarina, Greece. Wall painting; the *Prophet Elias*; twelfth century.

22 Vladimir, Russia. Wall painting; head of *Barlaam*; c. 1166.

24 Staraya Ladoga, Russia. Wall painting; *St George*; end of the twelfth century.

25 Spas Nereditsa, Russia. General view of the interior; end of the twelfth century.

26 Manuscript illumination; *St Mark*. Phillips Collection no. 3887; first half of the thirteenth century.

27 Manuscript illumination; the *Raising of Lazarus;* mid-thirteenth century. The Walters Art Gallery Baltimore, no. 10.531. century

dispelled the illusion that the Fourth Crusade brought anything other than destruction and disaster to the Byzantine world([9]).

But the views of Demus that the panel should be assigned to shortly before the end of the thirteenth century on the basis of its similarity to work in Kariye Camii – dated to the second decade of the fourteenth century – are better supported and are worthy of more serious consideration. He notes that the face of the Baptist is very close to that which appears among the paintings of the Parecclesion of Kariye Camii, done around 1320. The pose of the head is identical, the rendering of the hair follows similar lines, and the modelling of the face is executed in just the same way. It should be noted however that there is a difference in the eyes, which at Kariye are more severely conventionalised, so that the face is given a rather sly appearance, while in the Hagia Sophia mosaic they are rendered more naturally so that the expression is tender and compassionate. Demus also compares the Christ of Hagia Sophia to that of the *Deesis* in the inner narthex at Kariye, where Christ and the Virgin stand side by side above the smaller figures of Isaac Porphyrogenitus – a posthumous portrait – and the nun Melane (see p. 122). But close study shows that the head of Christ here is a good deal longer and narrower than that in Hagia Sophia, and is at the same time more stylised and more effeminate. The technique is also distinct, for the painterly, sfumato, character of the Christ in Hagia Sophia is not apparent in that at Kariye. Further the face of the Virgin at Kariye is less gentle and compassionate, the general effect rather harder. The Kariye mosaic is very lovely in itself, but it somehow appears weak beside that of the Hagia Sophia *Deesis*. In spite of its delicate intimacy, the Hagia Sophia mosaic at the same time reflects the grandeur and glory of old Byzantium, a spirit which was no longer present in the lighter, more picturesque work at Kariye.

Finally a suggestion has been put forward, though it has not so far been seriously argued, that the mosaic might have been set up during the Latin occupation of Constantinople between 1204 and 1261. At this time Hagia Sophia was a Roman Catholic, not an Orthodox cathedral, but the inscriptions on the mosaic are in Greek of a type that one would hardly associate with the Latin cult, while the theme of the *Deesis* is a wholly Orthodox one; it is inconceivable that a mosaic of this subject could have been set up in a church which, along with others in the city, had been converted to the Latin rite. Feeling between Christians of the Orthodox persuasion and the Latins was far from friendly([10]) and if members of the latter community wished to adorn one of their churches they would surely not have chosen a composition that in every way savoured of Orthodoxy, and they would surely have realised that the theme of the mosaic, 'Intercession', could to an Orthodox only have meant a prayer to be relieved from the oppression of the Latin domination! And apart from all this, the economic situation between 1204 and 1261 was hardly such as to have permitted the very considerable expenditure necessary to cover the cost of such a work, even if a Latin emperor could be thought of who would have favoured such a project.

Apart from questions of style, the nature of the social and political background should also be considered in any attempt to date the Hagia Sophia panel. In this connection it is hard to conceive of the *Deesis* mosaic as a product of the early Palaeologan age, done at a time when the emperors had hardly re-established themselves in the capital, and when such works as we know were done on behalf of the great nobles, not of the emperors. The whole character of the panel savours much more of the age before 1204. Even if the state was weak throughout the twelfth century, the Comnene emperors and their Court were bent on disguising the fact, and in their courtly actions they sought to maintain the magnificence of an older and grander age. Alexios Comnenos (1081–1118) was a considerable patron of art; his successor John (1118–43) set up the mosaic in Hagia Sophia which we have just noted, depicting himself and his queen. When the Crusaders conquered Constantinople in 1204, they stood amazed at the wealth and richness that confronted them. Surely the scale, the whole conception of the *Deesis* panel accords better with the pomp of the Comnene court than with the somewhat uncertain glory of the later thirteenth century? If the name of any individual is to be cited in association with it, that of John Comnenos, nicknamed the Good (1118–43), is the most likely. The mosaic depicting him and his queen is, it must be admitted, in a very different style, but the adjacent one of his son Alexios is much more personal and suggests that works in a progressive manner must have been produced simultaneously with more conservative ones.

The possibility that a work showing so humanistic a conception as that to the fore in the figures of the *Deesis* panel could have been set up as early as the middle of the twelfth century is borne out not only by the character of the icon *Our Lady of Vladimir*, to which we have already compared it, but also by the nature of the wall paintings at Nerez in Yugoslavia. They constitute the original decoration of a small but nevertheless elaborate church, set up under the patronage of a member of the Comnene family in 1164([11]). He must have employed an artist from the capital, for the style is wholly metropolitan, and the work is quite distinct from that of most of the other paintings of the age that we know in Yugoslavia, Greece or elsewhere, where provincial elements are prominent. Indeed most of the authorities are agreed as to the Constantinopolitan provenance of the painter of the Nerez frescoes, with the exception of Xyngopoulos, who thinks that he came from Salonica([12]). But though the evidence is scanty, there is reason to believe that the Salonican style had already assumed the more dramatic, more realist manner which was to characterise it in the fourteenth century.

The Nerez paintings are not only of special importance on account of their quality; they are also very fresh and experimental, and impress because of their essentially humanist sympathies and the interest shown throughout in personal characteristics and individual emotions. The isolated figures have thus lost much of the austerity of those of earlier date and stand out, like the old saint of uncertain identity illustrated on Plate 9, as men before whom one would not be embarrassed to confess one's sins or talk over one's troubles, and who would accord help and understanding to the erring human being. Again in the scenes of the Bible story the emotions of love and sympathy have a new part to play, there is a new freedom in the rendering and a new interest is shown in natural features. In the scene of the *Deposition* (Plate 10), for example, the Mother embraces the face of her beloved son, Nicodemus tenderly lowers the helpless but still supple body, St John is touched by an intimate, personal affection; nothing could be further removed from the austere symbolism of the rendering of the *Crucifixion* at Daphni than this wholly personal and intimate composition. The same approach characterises the *Lamentation*, in itself an emotional theme (Plate 11). The mother weeps unashamedly over her son's corpse; human affection has broken down the barriers of restraint. Neither of these scenes were usual in earlier Byzantine art, though the latter was to become in Italy after the fourteenth century the central theme of the whole iconographical cycle of the Passion([13]). At Nerez we see both of them for the first time playing the primary role that they were to assume in the fourteenth century in such a cycle as that presented by Giotto in the Arena chapel at Padua, and it is interesting to compare the iconography of the scenes, not so much because Giotto's renderings were well nigh identical with the earlier Byzantine ones, but rather because emotion is expressed at Nerez with just as much freedom as in Giotto's work (see Plate 75). At one time Giotto's paintings were believed to be wholly new and experimental in this respect.

In another of the scenes at Nerez, that of the *Nativity of the Virgin*, other new elements are to be noted (Plate 13 and 14). First we see not only a very serious attention being paid to human character, but also a new interest in nature for its own sake; one could find models for the faces of the midwives in any village of Macedonia or northern Greece today. There is, too, a new enquiry into problems of anatomy. True, the arm of the woman carrying in a jug to the spectator's right, is not very successfully articulated, but the painter was clearly experimenting with something new, in an effort to give life to his figures: he was not merely following an old-established model, but was seeking to depict and give expression to what he actually saw, with the object of escaping from the stereotyped renderings usual at an earlier age. An even more convincing illustration of this is to be seen if the two figures who are engaged in washing the child in the same scene are compared with the very similar ones who wash the Christ Child in earlier works. At Nerez they are strong, muscular peasants, who are shown by the painter working with energy and vigour: they may be contrasted with the more elegant, refined figures at Daphni, which are symbolic rather than real (see Plate 2).

Finished and balanced compositions, showing a new love of movement; expressive, vigorous, and living figures; essentially human emotions − these are the features we see at Nerez, though there was, too, a great feeling for monumentality, a true grandeur of conception, as in the rendering of the *Transfiguration* (Plate 8), which is particularly impressive and dignified. We see these same elements to the fore in the Hagia Sophia mosaic of the *Deesis* and in the icon *Our Lady of Vladimir*. All these works alike were precocious for their age, and all were well in advance of what was being done in Italy at the time [14]. Yet in the Byzantine world these features were rapidly becoming characteristic of the new metropolitan style which will be our theme throughout the rest of this book. We term it the Revival style to avoid the use of the more complicated and difficult word Renaissance.

In the absence of works other than the *Deesis* mosaic at Constantinople, our knowledge of the progress of change has to be based on the examination of the little that survives elsewhere, some of it done under the inspiration of the capital, some of it of a more provincial character. To this latter category belong the paintings at Kurbinovo, which must have been done by a local artist though they attest a very clear and marked debt to Nerez. They date from some 30 years later than Nerez − the year 1191 has been proposed. That they should show close iconographical similarities is not surprising, for the same models were of course frequently used throughout the Byzantine world. But in this case details are at times so closely similar that one can only conclude that the man who worked at Kurbinovo had actually been to Nerez and made notes of what he saw there. The depiction of St Pantaleimon supports this conclusion particularly clearly, for the carved marble frame which encloses the saint's figure at Nerez has been reproduced in paint at Kurbinovo (Plates 15 and 16). Other works there, like the *Transfiguration* and the *Lamentation*, are as closely akin (Plates 9, 11, 12 and 19) and at times even the facial types of Nerez were reproduced at Kurbinovo though the work there was cruder and the style more provincial (Plate 18). At Nerez we see the paintings of a master of great accomplishment, working in a very polished, sophisticated manner; at Kurbinovo the sophistication has been lost, though the lively approach which marked Nerez as a monument of the Revival style is quite clearly present, and scenes where an intimate human context has become almost too much exaggerated are added, as for example that of the Prophetess Anna giving suck to the infant Baptist. It has become almost violent in the search for realism and in the effort to render expression, especially with regard to the linear stylisation of the face [15] (Plate 18).

Another feature characteristic of the Kurbinovo paintings is to be seen in a love of angular, agitated movements, as for example in the garments of the angel of the *Annunciation* (Plate 17). Similar features appear in the costume of the same figure in the church of the Anargyroi at Kastoria, a few miles away across the present Greek frontier; it might almost have been done by the same painter. But the mannerism is to be found again around 1260 among the wall paintings of Hagia Sophia at Trebizond, nearly a thousand miles away (see p. 55). Happily in this instance a painting which serves to attest the existence of a common prototype is available in the form of an icon of the *Annunciation*, now in the monastery of St Catherine on Mount Sinai, but in all probability a work of the Constantinopolitan school, executed in the eighties of the twelfth century[16]. The Kurbinovo and Kastoria paintings represent a very provincial interpretation of a metropolitan model; that at Trebizond is rather more sophisticated and is closer to the Constantinopolitan original. Yet another derivative is to be found in a wall painting in the Panaghis tou Arakou at Lagoudhera in Cyprus; it is firmly dated to 1192. Other work of the same school is to be found at Perachorio in Cyprus; it is dated to 1191[17].

The lively style of the Nerez paintings would seem to have exercised an influence, though to a less marked degree, on certain other paintings in Macedonia; those at Manastir on Lake Prespa and at Markova Varos near Prilep may be noted. In other cases the influence may have been exercised more directly from Constantinople. Sometimes much of the original artistic quality was lost in the process of copying, as for example in most of the Cyprus paintings. But in other cases work of the very greatest beauty was produced, even though far away from the Byzantine capital. The mosaic decorations of Cefalù (1148 and later) and the Palatine Chapel at Palermo (from 1143) may be cited as instances of such an influence. The work belongs in the main to the monumental mid-Byzantine style. But in the Martorana at Palermo (*c.* 1148), even more at Monreale, there are indications that the Revival style was making its mark. The mosaics of the Martorana thus show a new lightness of touch and a new delicacy of feeling. Particularly interesting is the scene of the *Dormition of the Virgin* in the body of the church, which is particularly well conceived and very beautifully coloured. Indeed, the tender, delicate shades which are used here are perhaps the most distinctive feature of the work. Here, and even more in the scene of the *Presentation*, a markedly humanistic approach is to the fore (Plate 20), to be seen in the latter in the friendly way in which the high priest Simeon stretches out his hands to receive the child; the figure is intimate and personal and the sympathetic nature of its conception is quite distinct from what one would have encountered in the monumental art of an earlier date. At Monreale, towards the end of the century, the interest in life and personality has gone a good deal further; indeed at times it is rather exaggerated. There is less of tenderness and gentleness here, but more movement and expression.

Professor Kitzinger holds the view that the Monreale mosaics are to be grouped along with the paintings of Kurbinovo and Kastoria as outstanding examples of the new dynamic style[18]. But like the Macedonian paintings, they lack the delicacy

of the work at Nerez, and they are in many ways provincial rather than metropolitan. Nevertheless they are imbued with an astonishing vigour, which is well illustrated for example by the tremendous energy of the figures engaged in constructing the Ark or building the Tower of Babel (Plate 21). There is nothing dead or static about these scenes, while the way in which the costumes are broken up into what Kitzinger terms a 'multitude of cascading, zig-zagging, spiralling motifs which obscure both the actual design of the costume and the structure of the body wearing it', is surpassed only at Kurbinovo and Kastoria. A somewhat similar dramatic character is to be observed again in certain miniatures of the age, like those in copies of the Homilies of the Monk James in the Vatican (Gr. 1162) or the Bibliothèque Nationale (Gr. 1208)[19]. The illustrations of both these manuscripts are rather crude and perhaps somewhat over-forceful in contrast with Constantinopolitan originals, and they too must be counted as provincial works.

II. (opposite) Hagia Sophia, Constantinople. Detail of the Deesis Mosaic; Christ; mid-twelfth century.

Rather closer to Nerez are some fragmentary paintings at Djurdjevi Stupovi in Serbia (1168). They would seem to represent a fairly sophisticated stage of development, where the provincial exaggerations of Kurbinovo and Kastoria are absent. Paintings at Bačkovo in Bulgaria are also related, but they are a good deal more conservative, and similar restraint characterises the wholly Byzantine angel supporting a roundel bearing the Virgin at St Angelo in Formis in Italy[20]. This in some respects represents a manifestation of the new style, but it is both more accomplished and at the same time more conservative than are the paintings at Kurbinovo and Kastoria, and the same is true to some extent of work at Samarina in Greece recently published by Madame Sotiriou, which is both sophisticated and accomplished and again seems to be close to a Constantinopolitan model (Plate 23) [21].

Of all the paintings in the metropolitan style, however, the most important are certainly those in the Cathedral of St Demetrius at Vladimir in Russia, which date from between 1193 and 1197[22]. The lovely head of the Prophet Barlaam serves to indicate the quality of the detail (Plate 22). The figure belongs to a rendering of the *Last Judgement*. It is no provincial monument, and the elegance and beauty of the work show the Revival style at its best. The angels are of outstanding beauty, and the manner of their painting recalls the icon, *Our Lady of Vladimir*, done some sixty years earlier. The composition as a whole is elegant and refined; the Apostles are characterful and individual, and each stands out as a personality. Nowhere else at the end of the twelfth century is work of such beauty and distinction to be found, and we must assume that a Byzantine master of great accomplishment was closely involved with the production of their paintings.

The story that we traced in Macedonia seems to have been repeated here in Russia. The Vladimir paintings, like those at Nerez, are polished, sophisticated, metropolitan; others at Staraya Ladoga (1167) and Spas Nereditsa near Novgorod (1199), like those at Kurbinovo, are more provincial. Yet they are expressive and extremely forceful. At Staraya Ladoga the compositions are very dynamic and the individual figures, notably those of the apostles, have a strange, hypnotic gaze which is hardly paralleled elsewhere (Plate 24). Those at Spas Nereditsa are less individual (Plate 25); though there are resemblances to the *Last Judgement* at Vladimir, they are not as close as are those of Kurbinovo to those at Nerez, for local features are more to the fore, and it is possible to discern here a foretaste of the style that the painter Theophanes the Greek was to develop three centuries later in Novgorod and Moscow (see p. 165). The revival character of the work at Spas Nereditsa was originally noted by Millet, and both places were discussed by Kitzinger in connection with the progressive style of the Monreale mosaics. More recently

Lazarev has stressed the eastern affinities of the iconography, calling attention to links that bind them to Asia Minor[23]. Their destruction in the course of the Second World War represented the loss of what was probably the most complete monument of twelfth century painting in the East.

So far as the character of the more dramatic large-scale works like Monreale are concerned, Kitzinger is no doubt correct when he concludes that it is a mistake to speak here of 'Neo-Hellenism' or to find in this art the dawning of a new humanism (*Monreale*, p. 105). Though the masters there portrayed strong emotion they did so with an eye to the overall effect. But it may be questioned whether this conclusion is also valid with regard to certain other examples of the work of this age which we have been examining, notably the icon *Our Lady of Vladimir*, the *Deesis* mosaic in Hagia Sophia at Constantinople, the *Last Judgement* at Vladimir, and indeed most, if not all, of the paintings at Nerez. Here we are surely in the presence of works where a rather different end was in view, where a search to render tenderness, intimacy, delicacy and a profoundly human understanding plays a more important role than the love of dynamic movement and forceful expression that is so much to the fore at Monreale. In fact, we should distinguish two trends in the paintings of this twelfth-century Revival in the Byzantine world, the one vivid and forceful, with Monreale as its principal work, the other more intimate and restrained, exemplified by the Nerez paintings, the icon *Our Lady of Vladimir* and, if we are correct with regard to its date, the *Deesis* mosaic in Hagia Sophia.

In addition to the works noted above, we should probably assign to this family a Psalter in the Vatican (Vat. Palat. Gr. 381), which contains four miniatures; one shows *David Composing the Psalms* (f. IV), one *David Between Wisdom and Prophecy* (f. 2) (Plate 28), one *Moses Receiving the Law on Mount Sinai* (f. 169 v) and one *Moses Presenting the Law to the People* (f. 170). The landscape backgrounds to the Moses scenes are pictorial, the figures tall and elegant, but well modelled, with a definite feeling for sculptural form which savours of the classical. Indeed, on the page where David is depicted between Wisdom and Prophecy an old idea has been reborn, for the custom of portraying these abstract concepts in human form goes back to classical prototypes, while the figures themselves are treated in a very sculpturesque manner, being admirably modelled; they are possessed of something of the elegance of Attic work of the fourth century BC. Even if the monumentality has been lost and they are to be described as charming rather than grand, there is in them enough that savours of the ancient world, and at the same time enough that is both alive and new, to permit the application of the word 'Renaissance' to them in the fullest sense of the term. There has been some dispute as to the date of these illuminations, for Kondakov assigned the manuscript to the twelfth century, while others have suggested the fourteenth. As with the *Deesis* mosaic in Hagia Sophia it is hard to be certain, but a date towards the end of the twelfth century seems on the whole most likely[24].

If we can claim, as we hope, that a new style of art was born early in the twelfth century, there is some evidence to show that a comparable change was taking place in literature, though it was perhaps not quite so marked or so important as that in the visual arts — but then the visual arts were always more progressive and more significant in the Byzantine world than was the literature. As early as the eleventh century the revival of a neo-Platonic philosophy had begun to make itself felt as the result of the teaching of Psellus, who championed an outlook based on rational thought rather than on theology. His pantheistic views are reflected in the works of his pupil John Italus, writing of whom Setton says that he would seem to belong to the Italian quattrocento rather than to eleventh-century Byzantium[25]. Both the new ideas that Psellus propounded and the stress he laid on elegant style left a heritage behind them which was to bear fruit in literary developments in the twelfth century, even if the Platonist philosophy was condemned at the Councils of 1156 and 1157. The classics were still read with enthusiasm and were also newly edited and newly translated into Latin for the benefit of visitors from Italy[26]; new romances were evolved on the basis of classical themes, and new forms of writing were developed. One of the most outstanding figures was Theodore Prodromos, who produced satires and fiction of a very original type, notably a romance entitled *The War of the Cats and Mice*; it found popularity in the west, and formed there the subject of some rather Byzantinising frescoes at Purg in Austria. He also wrote a series of verses on the months. In a rather different vein the hagiographical writings of the tenth-century scholar Symeon Metaphrastes also exercised an effect, for they were imbued with a profound personal love for Christ, and their spirit runs parallel with the growth of the more humanistic, more compassionate, outlook in art. But most influential of all was the very experimental and original work of Anna Comnena, in her *Alexiad*, which was completed in 1148. Krumbacher terms it the first really important work of the literary renaissance which was to last through the Palaeologue age[27]. He describes Anna's style as humanist, though it also owed a dept to the classical world and more especially to Thucydides. But the very fact that a woman could write a lengthy work in fine prose devoted to the contemporary world and to the life of a single individual was an innovation of tremendous significance, as new in its own way as the frescoes of Nerez were in theirs.

In a short essay devoted to the origins of the thirteenth-century Renaissance in the Byzantine world in the literary field, Tuilier concludes that the developments that took place in the twelfth century cannot be counted as a Renaissance because knowledge of the classics had continued without interruption throughout the Macedonian age[28]. But this is to play with words. A taste for classical learning and classical literature may not have been greater in the twelfth than in the preceding two or three centuries, but new ideas were in the air, new literary forms were being created, and if we are not to term this a Renaissance we may nevertheless legitimately call it a Revival, and that word will be adhered to throughout the rest of this book as a general term to define the new art that was born with the twelfth century, and which saw its fullest developments in a series of very remarkable monuments set up all over the Byzantine world during the thirteenth.

It is impossible to believe that the essence of this style, so fresh, dynamic and expressive, could have been transplanted to the numerous widely separated regions in which we find it in any other way than as the result of the presence in those regions of actual artists; painters must have travelled in considerable numbers and with comparative ease. Such men, trained in the capital in the new manner, must have been present at Nerez, at Vladimir, at Monreale and even perhaps in Cyprus. In all these places their works were copied by local artists, with considerable skill by some of the apprentices at Monreale, with great understanding at Spas Nereditsa in Russia, and somewhat more clumsily at Kurbinovo and Kastoria. Model books might have served to inspire iconographical themes; only individuals could have transplanted this wholly distinct style; and so far as we can tell, it was in the Byzantine capital that it was first evolved, and thence that it was conveyed to serve as a basis for local developments in a whole series of widely dispersed regions.

2
Byzantine Painting in the Thirteenth Century

The essentially metropolitan character of the paintings at Nerez, Vladimir and elsewhere serves to indicate that artists from the capital were ready to venture far afield in the twelfth century, and the interest in humanism and personality that characterises work in both these places shows too that in these instances in any case the artists were amongst the most progressive and avant-garde of their day. In Sicily, on the other hand, the masters who worked on the great mosaic decorations of Cefalù and the Palatine Chapel, though no less competent, followed a more conservative trend in art, for there is little to distinguish their work from that which would, so far as we can judge, have been usual in the central parts of the Byzantine world towards the end of the great Macedonian age. However, the Sicilian masters must also have been trained in the Byzantine capital, for the metropolitan style, whether progressive or conservative, was quite distinct from the provincial, as we see it exemplified for instance at a fairly early date at Hosios Lukas, and at a later one at Kurbinovo and Kastoria.

A similar dispersal of artists from Constantinople seems to have distinguished the thirteenth century. Indeed, there is reason to believe that in addition to those who would have sought employment abroad in any case in order to satisfy the demands of patrons in Russia, the Balkans and elsewhere, many others fled the capital as a result of the Latin Conquest of 1204 because of their Orthodox faith, just as members of the leading families left the city for political reasons. The nobles gathered at Nicaea, in Epirus, and at far distant Trebizond, and soon new principalities, new states, were to come into being in those places that were wholly Greek and wholly Orthodox in character. Artists from Constantinople no doubt settled in these places also, while others went further afield and found employment with other patrons of Orthodox faith, especially the Slav princes in Bulgaria, Serbia, Macedonia and even Russia. It is thus in these peripheral areas that we must seek for examples of the metropolitan school in the thirteenth century rather than in the capital itself. There nothing is preserved, and it would seem unlikely that anything on a large scale was executed during the Latin occupation between 1204 and 1261, even if miniatures did at times continue to be produced.

Unfortunately we know little of what was being done in the two principal areas where the Greek Orthodox princes sought to reconstitute the empire, namely Nicaea and the Epirus, for at Nicaea nothing is preserved, while the important mosaics in the church of the Paragoritisa at Arta in Epirus are of much later date (*c.* 1290); paintings in smaller churches near Arta would mostly seem to be in a wholly provincial style. Nor are there any remains of this period in Salonica. It has, however, been proposed that a group of manuscripts may be isolated and associated with Nicaea([1]). The most important, and in any case the most lavishly illustrated example is the famous Rockefeller-McCormick manuscript at Chicago([2]) (No. 2400), but the so-called Gospels of Karahissar at Leningrad (Public Library Gr. 105), another Leningrad manuscript (Gr. 101), and two volumes in the Bibliothèque Nationale (Coislin 200 and Gr. 25), are akin([3]), and Buchthal has added to the group a previously unpublished copy of the Gospels formerly in the Phillipps collection (no. 3887) (Plate 26)([4]). Study of manuscripts included in the Byzantine Exhibition at Athens in 1964 permits the addition of several others to this list, notably a New Testament and Psalter at Palermo (Museo 4) and another in the British Museum (Add. 11836), while a copy of the New Testament in the Library of the Greek Patriarchate at Jerusalem (No. A. T. 37) is also akin, though of higher quality than most of the others([5]). Buchtal suggests a date quite early in the century for most of these manuscripts, and there seems good reason to accept his conclusion.

Another interesting manuscript, which has sometimes been attributed to the twelfth and sometimes to the fourteenth century, is a copy of the Gospels in the Walters Art Gallery at Baltimore (No. 10.531); it too should surely be assigned to the thirteenth century (Plate 27). It contains portraits of three of the Evangelists – the fourth is missing – with, opposite St Mark, the *Baptism*; opposite St Luke, the *Annunciation*; and opposite St John, the *Raising of Lazarus*. The style of its miniatures is however close to that of the wall paintings in Hagia Sophia at Trebizond, and as the manuscript is associated with that city historically, it seems likely that it was illuminated there. The city was certainly an important centre at the time, for two princes of the Comnene family established there in 1204 an empire which was to survive in independence till 1461, and throughout the whole of this period it appears to have been a significant centre of art production.

As yet we know of no manuscripts that can be definitely assigned to Salonica, nor are there any major works of art there that can be dated to the thirteenth century, even though the city was freed from the Latins before 1225. It would seem, however, that scriptoria may have continued to exist in Constantinople even during the Latin domination and one or two manuscripts, notably one in the British Museum (Burney 20), were done there very soon after the restoration of Orthodoxy in 1261([6]).

It would thus seem that quite a number of schools of illumination existed, but even though the various examples we know show a certain degree of variation in style, the work was all, broadly speaking, in what may be termed a metropolitan manner, and it is all in a general way similar to that of the remarkable series of wall paintings in the monastery church of Mileševa in Serbia, done under the patronage of King Vladislav between 1230 and 1237. The paintings are signed, near a figure of St Demetrius, by three painters, Demetrius, George and Theodore([7]). Radojčić claims that they were Serbs, but the style suggests that in any case the leading master was a Greek. The king is depicted twice, once on the north wall of the narthex, and once on the south wall, in each case holding a model of the church. The latter rendering is the more intimate and is clearly a portrait from the life (Plate 31). Though religious subjects were always treated with a more rigorous convention than secular ones, the artist seems to have wanted to introduce the same human element that characterises the portrait of the king into his rendering of the religious themes. In any case the faces of the mourners in the scene of the death of the Virgin suggest this, for they are expressive and individual.

It is, however, in the depiction of the Maries at the Sepulchre that the Revival style is most clearly illustrated (Plates VIII and 30). The timorous figures of the Maries are expressive and alive, but most striking is the way in which the sleeping soldiers who guarded the tomb are shown (Plate IX). Their armour and helmets are depicted with the greatest realism, and would seem to follow a model of the day rather than any old and long established convention, where classical costumes were usual. Yet the angel is a figure of almost classical majesty, and may be compared to that of the eighth century in Santa Maria Antiqua at Rome, which has always been signalled out as a striking example of the survival of the classical style in Early Christian Art[8]. In fact the Angel at Mileševa justifies the application of the term Renaissance to the art of this age perhaps more than any other figure, for in it are blended both hints of a new humanism and features that indicate a return to the spirit of the antique. The way in which the scene is shown is also interesting, for the Resurrection was usually rendered in Byzantine art by the scene where Christ raises up Adam and Eve from the tomb, with the broken gates of limbo at His feet; the empty tomb was more usual in the west. But there are eastern prototypes for the Mileševa rendering, as for example in paintings at Karabaş Kilisse in Cappadocia which date from 1061.

The humanistic understanding which characterises the rendering of the sleeping soldiers is carried even further in the scenes of the *Deposition* (Plate VI) and the now fragmentary *Entry into Jerusalem* (Plate VII); both are particularly effective, especially with regard to the colouring. The *Annunciation* is one of the most intimate and enchanting conceptions of the subject that is to be found prior to the development of Sienese painting more than a century later (Plate 32). Nowhere else, even in Gothic art, is so gentle, timid and charming a figure of the Virgin to be found. The *Deposition* is more full of emotion, yet it too is tender and delicate, and represents a continuation of the style that we noted some seventy years earlier at Nerez. The later date of the Mileševa painting is attested by the greater elaboration of the scene and the inclusion of a number of additional figures. It is, however, clearly derived from a Constantinopolitan prototype in the Revival style, and even if some of the other scenes do suggest the possibility of some influence from Gothic art of the West, the general character of the Mileševa paintings is essentially Byzantine.

One idiosyncrasy in these paintings may be noted which occurs again at Sopoćani, and bears out the basically metropolitan character of both decorations; in some of the scenes the backgrounds are coloured yellow and a series of intercrossing lines are drawn over them, presumably to represent mosaic cubes. The painter must thus have had some mosaic model in mind, and the most likely source for such a model would have been in metropolitan court art. In the narthex, on the other hand, the backgrounds are blue, and the subject matter and style of the work are quite distinct, for in place of majestic scenes from Christ's life we find portraits of saints and anchorites. The painters who worked in this part of the church must have been monks; the subject matter of their work was dictated by their theological preoccupations, and the paintings are to be assigned to a quite distinct monastic school. Yet their quality is still high, and the work is sophisticated even if less polished than that of the Christological cycle. Further, the compositions here are effective and dramatic, as for example in the scene of the *Betrayal of Our Lord* (Plate 33) − a rendering which is very close to it is to be found in the upper church at Assisi, which is usually attributed to a follower of Cimabue, and must date from the last quarter of the thirteenth century[9].

Yet a third group of painters worked in the exo-narthex where St Sava was buried. They were responsible for an elaborate rendering of the *Last Judgement*,

III Trebizond, Church
of Hagia Sophia. Wall
painting; south-east
pendentive of the
dome. Detail of Christ
from the scene of the
Anastasis; c. 1260

done probably in 1243. This work is more dramatic than the rest of that at Mileševa, but also somewhat less accomplished; it can perhaps hardly be described as metropolitan, yet it reflects the life and vigour of the new style even if it is lacking in polish; the rendering of angels driving groups of false prophets and unjust kings to hell is characteristic (Plate 29). Its vigour and spirit suggest that the painter responsible may well have been a pupil of the master of the main decoration; the former was either a Greek from Constantinople or a Serb who had been trained in the metropolis; the latter was almost certainly a local painter[10].

The next series of paintings that display the influence of the metropolitan school are some thirty years later in date. They are in the monastery church of Sopoćani, founded by King Stephen Uros I around 1265. Here the work is grand and monumental, but is at the same time possessed of great elegance and refinement, and is distinguished by a particularly developed feeling for colour; the shades are blended with outstanding skill, violets alternating with green, blue with yellow or ochre, with the most lovely effect. The modelling is subtly accomplished by building up the darker tones above the outline, as in the face of the young St John (Plate XI). Much the same system was, as we shall see, employed in Hagia Sophia at Trebizond, and the rendering of the individual figures reveals a definite relationship of tradition though the details of workmanship are distinct.

Taken as a whole, the paintings in the body of the church at Sopoćani are probably better preserved than any others of the thirteenth century in the Byzantine world, both with regard to the number of scenes available for study, and in respect of their actual condition.

Nowhere else are the colours quite so lovely or so satisfying, nowhere else are the figures quite so impressive. The numerous single figures which adorn not only the lowest register of the walls but also the upper ones on the four pilasters that support the dome are amazingly grand and dignified, while the scenes are expressive and beautifully composed. The great *Dormition of the Virgin* on the west wall is especially effective (Plate 34). The composition is extremely full — a vast crowd of mourners in the foreground, elaborate buildings and further figures behind, and in the sky groups of angels supported on clouds. The mourners are sorrowful and the event is conducted with all the emotion of an eastern funeral — note, for example, the wailing women on the balcony. Yet at the same time it is a joyous occasion; the Virgin's soul is received by Christ and conveyed to heaven; after-life is safeguarded, resurrection assured, and as much as any painting I know this composition attests the whole essence of this part of the Christian belief. It offers us a moving illustration and a powerful allegory of the faith at the same time.

There was a very full cycle of scenes from our Lord's life at Sopoćani, and many of them are still well preserved. The *Nativity* on the northern wall is in part rather battered, but the shepherds who receive the news of our Lord's birth are complete and very expressive; the figure of an old man, left for the moment bemused, while his younger companion seeks to explain the situation to him, is especially striking (Plate 46). Equally alive are the midwives who prepare the Child's bath on the opposite side of the composition (Plate 41).

More experimental is the scene that stands opposite to it, *Christ teaching in the Temple*, for the artist has obviously been much concerned with the rendering of the architecture (Plate 35). His system of perspective was that usual in Byzantine art, for it is inverted, but the sense of depth is very satisfactorily conveyed, and the whole composition is convincing even to an eye accustomed to the wholly different conventions usual in the west. Indeed, the painter was very much of a master at

dealing with architecture, and gave prominence to it in some of the other scenes, as for example in the *Dormition*. In the scene of *Christ's Appearance to the Apostles in the Closed Rooms* on the north wall of the Sanctuary the architecture is more conventional, but the figure of Christ is very lovely and very expressive (Plate 36) and the same is true of the rendering of the *Doubting Thomas* (Plate X). His appearance to the two Maries on the opposite wall is, on the other hand, amazingly progressive, for the modelling of the figures of the two women, their massive sculpturesque forms, and the three-quarter or even completely side-face treatment seem to herald the art of Giotto (Plate 37). The women mourners in the *Deposition* in his paintings in the Arena chapel at Padua clearly echo those at Sopoćani. The basic arrangement of the composition however perhaps derives from an earlier model, for one of the miniatures in the Bible of Leo in the Vatican (Reg. 1) shows St Nicholas and two donors in much the same pose[11].

As regards beauty of colouring, originality of conception, grandeur of proportions and effectiveness of composition, the paintings in the body of the church at Sopoćani are to be counted among the finest of mediaeval times, and the metropolitan character of the work is again not to be disputed[12]. The reticent majesty of the figures in the apse is especially striking (Plate XIII), and it is hard to believe that anything finer or more beautiful could have been produced even in Byzantium itself; in fact the paintings of Mileševa and Sopoćani show that the members of the Nemanja family were patrons of the greatest discernment, able to assemble for their service some of the foremost artists of the whole Byzantine world.

The paintings in the narthex and the side chapels, though of the same date as those in the body of the church, are more monastic in character and are to be assigned to a different workshop. The poses are less elegant, less monumental, the modelling less accomplished and the colours less effectively blended. Instead the figures are short and dumpy and in the faces attention is concentrated on inward expression rather than on outward beauty. The hands of several painters are to be distinguished, the best of them perhaps being the man who was responsible for the scene of the *Death of Stephen Nemanja* in the chapel on the south side at the western end (Plate 39). He was a master of the pathetic of very great ability, his figures are alive and very expressive, and his rendering of the scene is moving and compelling even if the wonderful rhythmical movement of the figures in the body of the church is absent. His palette again was rather more sombre and the colours less varied. Works in the narthex, where the *Last Judgement* appears on the north wall, the *Tree of Jesse* on the south and the *Story of Joseph* on the west, are vivid and expressive, but it is less grand than the main decoration, though all the scenes are to be assigned to much the same date. The paintings in the side chapels and exo-narthex are mostly later[13], but there is a very effective rendering of the *Annunciation* in the prothesis (Plate 40).

Close in style to the paintings in the body of the church at Sopoćani, and done at much the same date, are those which decorate a little chapel dedicated to the Trinity which stands alone, not far from the monastery of Chilandari on Mount Athos. These paintings have only recently been noticed[14]. They are in a very battered state, but enough survives to show that they were in a grand and monumental style; the faces are elaborately modelled and are of a distinctly classical character, and they belong to the metropolitan trend in art. As far as it is possible to judge from monochrome reproductions the work seems to be closely related to that at Sopoćani, and an artist trained there may well have worked at Chilandari for it was a Serbian monastery and close contacts were always maintained with the mother country.

IV Trebizond, Church of Hagia Sophia. Wall painting; detail from the *Feeding of the Five Thousand*; c. 1260.

V Trebizond, Church of Hagia Sophia. Wall painting; *Casting out of a Devil from the Daughter of the Woman of Canaan;* c. 1260.

Though the paintings of Mileševa and Sopoćani are certainly the most outstanding of all those that survive in Yugoslavia, certain other decorations of the thirteenth century are likewise of very high quality and are also to be classed as basically of the metropolitan family, even if local elements are more to the fore or if they are clearly to be attributed to different painters or to different workshops. Once more they attest the perspicacity of the patrons who were able to sponsor so many artists of varied outlook, all of whom were able to produce work that can never for a moment be condemned as provincial. Most important probably is the decoration of the central one of the three churches that form the Patriarchate at Peć, that dedicated to the Holy Apostles (Plate 43). It was set up by Abbot Arsenije I shortly before 1250 and was decorated between then and 1263, whereas the paintings in the adjacent churches to north and south belong to the fourteenth century. The paintings have recently been cleaned, and though those in the central church are rather more sombre than those at Sopoćani, the backgrounds being deep blue instead of yellow or some pale colour and the colours generally darker, they are nevertheless possessed of great grandeur and dignity, and again bear witness to the non-provincial character of the best Serbian art of the thirteenth century. The same is true of the rather fragmentary decoration of Gradać (Plate 42), dating from 1276, of a painting of the Archangel Michael in a cave chapel near Struga, and to a lesser degree of the extensive decoration of the church at Arilje, dating from 1296 (Plate 44). The Gradać paintings are in a light, rather picturesque vein, and are gay rather than impressive. The old shepherd in the *Nativity* scene, for instance, has great charm. The Struga angel, which has only recently been published[15], is grander and more monumental, and its style suggests a comparison with a fine icon of the Crucifixion now preserved at Ochrid which should perhaps be attributed to the Sopoćani school[16]; it dates from the second half of the thirteenth century.

The universal character of this style is attested if paintings in the church of St Nicholas at Geraki in Greece are compared, for they are clearly related (Plates 47 and 48); Madame Sotiriou has indeed noted their similarity to those at Gradać[17]. Both are to be counted as fairly pure examples of the Metropolitan style, whereas the work at Arilje is more truly Serbian; it shows a greater concern with picturesque detail, the movements are more dynamic, and greater stress is laid on expression. Indeed one can see at Arilje a foretaste of the manner that was to become widespread in southern Serbia and northern Macedonia around 1300, which was designated by Millet as the 'Macedonian' and has, more narrowly, been described as the School of Milutin. It is believed by some to have resulted from the workings of a national Slav element, while others would attribute its birth to the influence of Salonica.

The work of a wholly distinct, but none the less progressive, school is to be distinguished in certain other decorations, notably that of the great church of the Virgin in the Monastery of Studenica, built just before 1200 for Stephen Nemanja, and decorated in 1208. The superb *Crucifixion* on the west wall there is most important (Plates 45 and 49). The individual figures are all particularly well done, the work is precise and careful, and the faces are full of life and essentially personal; the centurion who stands immediately behind St John is especially expressive. There are three women behind the Virgin, but the last of them is the work of a later restorer. The actual Crucifixion itself is rendered with very profound feeling, the emotion of the scene being intensified by the rather sombre colouring. The faces are of a curious yellow tone which is not known elsewhere, the background blue, with gold stars on it. The rendering of Christ's head, with eyes closed in death, is something new in Byzantine art, but it occurs again in a closely similar rendering of the same scene at Žiča, done between 1219 and 1230 (Plate 55); were it not for this, it would be tempting to assign the Studenica painting to a later date. In neither case is the work wholly Byzantine in style, and both renderings may be compared with a wooden cross by Giunta Pisano in the Church in Santa Maria degli Angeli at Assisi dated to around 1250 (Plate 50). Giunta Pisano was supposedly born around 1202 and died about 1258, so that the Serbian paintings both antedate the Italian panel, which was cited by Grondijs as the earliest examples known to him of the theme of the dead Christ on the cross[18].

The similarity of the renderings at Studenica and Žiča on the one hand and the Italian panels on the other suggests some sort of definite link between the two areas. Radojčić sought to explain it by attributing the Yugoslav work to what he termed 'pictores Graeci' — painters of the Orthodox faith working on the Adriatic coast in what may be termed a Byzanto-Italian style — but this does not really solve the problem, for the work of these painters, so far as we know it, was much clumsier than that at Studenica and most of it is to be attributed to a later date. Nor was the rendering of Christ with bent head and closed eyes fully developed in Italy till well on in the thirteenth century. Indeed the painting at Studenica is one of the earliest examples of the theme that we know, and even if it occurs earlier in Germany, as in the Gero and Werden Crucifixions, it must, for the moment, be regarded as the source from which the new type spread to the Italo-Byzantine area. Yet the style is not Byzantine even if the iconographical theme had by the next century become fairly usual in the Byzantine world. There is a similar head at Staro Nagoričino (1317) and Xyngopoulos has also compared renderings at Kalabaca and Servia in northern Greece, denying any Italian influence in either case[19]. His comparisons are convincing, though the Greek work is cruder and lacks the polish of that at Studenica. These paintings were no doubt done by a man trained at Salonica, and it is possible that the artists responsible for the Studenica and the Žiča Crucifixions came from there also; this would in any case serve to explain the stylistic differences between these paintings and the work of the monumental group which we see at Mileševa, Sopoćani and elsewhere, where the links were undoubtedly with Constantinople.

Besides the Crucifixion there are at Žiča vestiges of an extensive decoration of the early fourteenth century in a more truly Byzantine style, and the records suggest that painters were brought from Constantinople by Archbishop Sava III to undertake the work. In some of the scenes there is a tremendous mass of details, as for example in that of the *Dormition of the Virgin* (Plate 56), where there is not only a profusion of figures in the foreground, but also a very elaborate architectural composition behind, while the whole sky is occupied by groups of figures framed by and supported on clouds, a mannerism which el Greco was to copy three centuries later. But though the style is basically metropolitan, it is a different art that we see here, where a mass of elaborations and a new interest in picturesque detail have become the concern of the artists, rather than grandeur of presentation and profundity of interpretation.

In addition to the decorations noted above which are all to a greater or lesser degree in what may be termed the grand manner, there were of course also a number of local schools at work; that of Raska was the most important of them in the north, while in Macedonia several other groups of paintings may be distinguished, notably one recently discovered at Manastir. Several painters appear to have worked there, one of them in a very conservative style and another in a manner which

VI Mileševa, Serbia.
Wall painting; the
Deposition; c. 1235.

VII Mileševa, Serbia.
Wall painting; the
Entry into Jerusalem.
c. 1235.

VIII Mileševa, Serbia.
Wall painting; the
*Maries at the
Sepulchre*; c. 1235.

must have been inspired by Kurbinovo; all the work apparently dates from 1271[20].

Other local schools were also in existence in Bulgaria, but the most outstanding of the thirteenth-century paintings there, those at Boiana near Sofia, are a good deal more sophisticated, and though they can hardly be classed along with the metropolitan groups in Serbia, they do nevertheless show links with Constantinople and in their humanism and vividity, bear witness to the widespread nature of the Revival style.

The Boiana paintings are firmly dated to 1259, and the inscriptions that accompany the scenes are in Bulgarian. The compositions follow Greek models so far as iconography is concerned, and certain scenes from the life of St Nicholas, which is fully illustrated, belong to a tradition associated with the Byzantine capital[21]. But in the most important part of the work from the artistic point of view, which is to be found in the paintings that deal with the life of Christ, the figures are treated with a degree of intimacy that is quite distinct; particularly noteworthy is the figure of *Christ Euergetes* (Benefactor) at the east end (Plate 53). His expression is tender, his character human and personal; it may be contrasted with a typical work of the Second Golden Age like that at Hosios Lukas in Greece, where a more austere, much less personal conception is to the fore. More typical of the Revival style as a whole however is the scene of *Christ Teaching in the Temple* (Plate 54), for there an elaborate architectural background to the scene is included, the youthful Christ follows a wholly human, essentially personal type, while the doctors are all individuals of character and personality.

Another interesting feature of the Boiana paintings are the portraits of the donors, the Sevastocrator Kaloyan and his consort Dessislava (Plates 51 and 52). They are clothed in costumes of the finest material, Dessislava's robe is of a rich figured Byzantine silk and it would seem that the textiles of which these costumes were made must have been Constantinopolitan products. More significant so far as a study of the Revival is concerned, however, is the close attention that the artist must have paid to his models when he painted them; the obvious interest in the personality of the figures alone affords an instance of the contacts that the painters of this age must have maintained with everyday life. The same is true of the portraits of the Tsar Constantine Asen and his Queen Irene, though they are rather more imperial and less personal; even St Theodore is rendered in a very individual manner. There may have been more than one painter at work at Boiana, but if this was so, all must have been trained in the same school and all alike were imbued with the spirit of the Revival, though they interpreted it in a way which can only be defined as a Bulgarian variant.

Some of the paintings at Tirnovo again show a new interest in life and movement, while those of angels that originally decorated the dome of the church of St George at Sofia have much of the monumentality and grandeur of the works at Sopoćani. Something of the same character appears in the rather later paintings of the prophets which were placed above them in the fourteenth century (Plate 59[22]). Many of them show the same grand and forceful characteristics as are to be found in Yugoslavia, and the work is to be counted as some of the most interesting in the Balkans, in spite of its very poor state of preservation.

The paintings at Boiana represent a local, but very important, school that seems to have developed in Bulgaria on the basis of ideas drawn from Constantinople; those in St George's church at Sofia are closer to Sopoćani, and must be counted as examples of the universal metropolitan group of which the paintings at Mileševa and Sopoćani are the most important examples in the Balkans. But other paintings,

also metropolitan in character, have recently been discovered at the opposite end of the Byzantine world, in the church of Hagia Sophia at far distant Trebizond, where rulers of the Comnene line had established an independent empire at the time of the Latin conquest of Constantinople in 1204.

The church that they decorate stands some three miles to the west of the town on a high promontory overlooking the Black Sea([23]). It is a fine building, constructed of neatly squared stones and furnished with large porches on the north, west, and south sides, which give it the appearance of a cruciform building, though inside it takes the form of the normal three-aisled, cross-in-square church with dome upheld on four marble columns. It became a mosque early in the seventeenth century, at which time the wall paintings were whitewashed over, and when Texier and a number of other western travellers visited the church around the middle of the nineteenth century the paintings could just be discerned below the whitewash. In a few places more was visible, and a portrait of the emperor Manuel I of Trebizond (1238–63) was noted by Finlay; accompanying it was an inscription giving the emperor's name and titles and describing him as the 'founder' of the church. On the basis of this, as well as on the evidence of some of the sculptures on the exterior, the church may be dated to his reign, and as a careful examination of the paintings has shown that those now visible were the first to be set on the walls, there seems good reason to believe that they too must be assigned to the same period. A date around 1260 seems probable for those in the church itself. Those in the narthex may perhaps be rather later, but they are still to be attributed to the third quarter of the thirteenth century, and the same men who worked in the church must have been responsible for them.

If only the paintings could have been cleaned at the time that Finlay saw the portrait, a great deal would no doubt prove to have been preserved. As it was, the building was restored as a mosque towards the end of the nineteenth century by a rich and pious Moslem; where the plaster bearing the paintings was fragile it was wholly removed, and where it was firm it was hacked to facilitate the adherence of a new layer of plaster above. The unpleasant holes that were left by this process have now been filled and the paintings toned in over the filling, so that the general effect is not spoilt; the toning in can however be distinguished from close to. The result of the Moslem restoration was to destroy in great part what must, only a hundred years ago, have been one of the most complete examples of thirteenth century Byzantine painting available. But nevertheless, certain scenes do survive in the church itself and in the north porch and the narthex they are much better preserved.

In the apse the Virgin is shown enthroned between the Archangels Gabriel and Michael, the Child on her knee. The composition was a usual one for this position, and the rendering here is in a style very close to that at Boiana in Bulgaria, firmly dated to 1259. On the vault of the Presbytery is the *Ascension*, Christ before a mandorla or glory, upheld by four angels at the corners, with two more at the sides, blowing trumpets; below stand the Apostles, six on each side, gazing in wonder at the manifestation above. The figure of Christ is closely related to one in a rock-cut chapel at Ivanovo in Bulgaria known as the Gospodov Dol (Plate 58); it is to be assigned to much the same date as the Trebizond paintings, in opposition to those in the better known chapel at the same place, where the work dates from the fourteenth century (see p. 152)([24]).

At a lower level, on the vertical walls at either side, were scenes from the Resurrection cycle, the *Incredulity of Thomas, Christ's appearance on the shores of Lake*

IX Mileševa, Serbia. Wall painting; detail of *Sleeping Soldiers* from the *Maries at the Sepulchre*; c. 1235.

Tiberias (Plate 60), and the *Mission of the Apostles*. The colours are of real beauty, and the figures expressive. The poses too are varied, some of them more complicated than was usual in Byzantine art. Most interesting however is the great attention which was paid to the anatomy of the figures and the musculature of the limbs. The muscles are rendered with much greater realism, and the figures with a closer observation of nature than is usual in Byzantine work of the period. Only in some of the scenes at Nerez such as that of the *Washing of the Child* is anything at all comparable to be found.

Some of the best preserved of the paintings in the church itself are those in the dome. The *Pantocrator* occupies the summit, the apostles the twelve spaces between the windows of the drum (Plate 66), the prophets the window embrasures and a great *Choir of Angels* the area above this – a sort of upper drum situated between the actual dome and the windows below. This frieze was of great beauty, an impressive composition containing little short of 100 figures; 79 actually survive (Plate 57). The colours are rich; the faces, where they are preserved, very beautiful. The manner of painting can be clearly discerned; the general lines were first painted fairly thinly in red, on the damp plaster, and the details were then built up above this ground, the heavier colours first, the highlights last; by the time the modelling of the features was done, the plaster was more or less dry. In the faces there was usually a green, *terra verde*, undercoat on which the flesh tints were imposed, often in several layers. The manner of painting employed at Sopoćani was similar, but there *terra verde* had a less important role to play as undercoat. Its intensive use was perhaps a peculiarity of the Trebizond region, for it characterised some Armenian paintings of the seventeenth century which were preserved in the monastery of Kaimakli near the city until 1920, but which have now been destroyed. Green undercoats also seem to have been very popular in Georgia, both for wall paintings and icons.

The paintings in the four pendentives are rather unusual, for each contains both a scene – as in the system followed at Hosios Lukas, Daphni and many other places in the Byzantine world – and an Evangelist – as at Nicaea and in many churches in Greece and on Mount Athos; nowhere else, to the writer's knowledge, are the two systems of pendentive decoration – that is the Evangelist and a scene – combined as they are in Hagia Sophia at Trebizond. There the *Nativity* occupies the north-western pendentive, together with *St Luke*; the *Baptism*, with *St Mark*, is to the south-west (Plate 61), the *Crucifixion* with *St Matthew* to the north-east, and the *Anastasis*, with *St John*, to the south-east (Plate III). In the rendering of two of these figures a curious feature is to be noted, for the evangelist identified by the accompanying inscription as St Mark actually has St John's emblem, the eagle, while St John has St Mark's, the lion. Either the painter made a mistake, or he chose to follow some other system[25]; there is no doubt as to the identity of the figures. The paintings in the pendentives are somewhat battered, but the colours are of great beauty, and the faces profound and expressive; enough survives to attest the very high quality and accomplished style of the work.

Happily the paintings of the narthex are more complete than those in the body of the church, and quite a number of scenes from Christ's life are well preserved; some of them are rather unusual and they are not even all included in the very full cycles like that in the mosaics of Kariye Camii at Constantinople. The *Marriage at Cana* is a large, elaborate composition, full of vividness and spirit (Plate 62). A fairly rigid hierarchical system, where the figures of lesser importance are shown on a progressively smaller scale than the more important, has been retained here –

witness the minute serving maid carrying in an immense dish at the door. The elaborate architectural background and the gay hanging at the back, indicating that the event takes place indoors, are however, wholly characteristic of the Revival style, and the old man stroking his chin and holding his wine glass up to the light is particularly vivid. The same decorative architecture appears in the scene of *Christ among the Doctors*, and there are the same distinctions of scale in the figures, though the general effect is more static. But the expressions are vivid and their import is borne out by the poses and gestures, notably the wonder of the doctors and the anxious surprise of the parents.

These scenes are comparatively restricted in scale, but on the upper part of the northern wall and on the eastern slope of the adjacent vault is one which is given unusual prominence — the *Feeding of the Five Thousand* (Plates 63 and 64). It is shown in far greater detail than is usual; the apostles, the baskets for the remains, the people seated in groups to receive their food — all are there, and the individuals are rendered with a vividness and interest in life which is quite exceptional. Some of the figures, one might think, were modelled on men who could have been met with in the town of Trebizond — some might even be seen in the bazaars there today; they have very much the appearance of Lazes, a people of distinctive physical type who inhabit the coastal area between Trebizond and Georgia (Plate IV).

One of the most unusual and impressive of the scenes in the narthex is that of the *Casting out of a Devil from the Daughter of the Woman of Canaan*, a scene very rarely depicted in Orthodox iconography (Plate V). Here the artist's skill in the rendering of vivid, expressive emotions has been given free rein, and the anxious care of the mother and the rigid, apoplectic pose of the child have been conveyed with particular success. It is perhaps the most expressive of the paintings, but is no doubt to be assigned to the same hand as the *Feeding of the Five Thousand*, where the same liveliness and power of expression are to be seen. Some of the other scenes are rather more conventional, like those from the Old Testament in the North Porch, though even here the work is spirited and the individual faces are rendered with very great skill (Plate 65).

Another interesting scene is the *Annunciation* over the door into the main body of the church, for the fussy folds of the angels' costume follow a very distinct mannerism, and suggest a comparison with the work at Kurbinovo or Kastoria in Macedonia, done more than half a century earlier. We have already noted that this manner also no doubt stemmed from Constantinople, a supposition which is supported by an icon of the same scene recently published by Professor Weitzmann, which is to be dated to the latter part of the twelfth century and would appear to have been the work of a Constantinopolitan painter[26].

In addition to the wall paintings there are a few works of a portable character of thirteenth-century date which should perhaps be mentioned at this stage. The earliest of them is a miniature mosaic of the *Crucifixion* now at Berlin. It has sometimes been regarded as a Sicilian product and dated to the twelfth century; even if it was produced in Sicily it bears the stamp of the metropolitan school; a date early in the thirteenth century seems more likely[27]. To Sicily itself, on the other hand, are probably to be assigned two panels in the National Gallery at Washington (Plate 67); they look like icons, but there are definite Italian elements, notably in the treatment of the eyes — in Italy the eyes are invariably shown half-closed and the flesh below them fades gently into the flat cheek; in Byzantine renderings there is a lower lid and then a patch of light. The panels are probably to be assigned to some local workshop where Italian and Byzantine elements had been blended together to produce a composite style of provincial character, much as they were blended in the so-called 'Crusading' school of miniature painting[28].

The existence of this school has only recently been established by Buchthal with regard to the manuscripts and Weitzmann with regard to panel paintings, thanks to discoveries made by him on Mount Sinai. These Crusading paintings show a curious mixture of influences; a Byzantine system of iconography is followed, but the style, though basically Byzantine, also shows very distinct Italian and French elements, to be seen in such general characteristics as a new interest in movement and a greater love of emotion, and in a more particular manner in the large clumsy heads and a curious roving expression in the eyes. Weitzmann suggests that the icons were produced by westerners, some of them French and some Italian, who had to a great extent, though not wholly, assimilated the Byzantine idiom[29], and the same was probably true of the miniature painters. He locates the school in Acre and assigns its products to the second half of the thirteenth century; some of the miniatures were done at a rather earlier date. The school is an unusual and an extremely interesting one, though it must be regarded as essentially peripheral. Many of its products, however, are in the same mixed style as the wall paintings of 1208 at Studenica, mentioned above, where an almost identical blend of eastern and western elements is to be found; the Studenica paintings, however, show no links with France, but are clearly akin to the work of Giunta Pisano in Italy.

In summarising the character of Byzantine painting in the thirteenth century it may be said that in its search for vividness, in its interest in expression and in its general humanism, painting in the Byzantine world had travelled a very long way from the severely formal style of mid-Byzantine times − very much further indeed than had painting in Italy during the same century − and if the paintings of Mileš-eva, Sopoćani and Trebizond are to be taken as a true gauge of the best work of the period, the quality of the paintings of what we have termed the Metropolitan group was just as high as that of the best Italian work done half a century later. The paintings of the Byzantine Revival in the thirteenth century in fact represent a natural continuation of the developments that began in the twelfth, and if progress in Constantinople was brought to a stop as a result of the Latin conquest in 1204, it continued elsewhere in a most brilliant, accomplished and sophisticated way, to produce in the thirteenth century a school of fundamental importance in the story of western art. It is a school which was wholly unfamiliar to past generations of art historians; and is still truly appreciated only by specialists, it should not be overlooked by anyone interested in the early developments of western painting.

29 (above) Mileševa, Serbia. Wall painting; *Angel Driving the Unjust Kings to Hell*; c. 1235.

30 (right) Mileševa, Serbia. Wall painting; head of *Angel of the Resurrection*; c. 1235.

31 Mileševa, Serbia. Wall painting; head of *King Vladislav*; c. 1235.

32 Mileševa, Serbia. Wall painting; *Virgin*, in the scene of the Annunciation; c. 1235.

33 *(opposite)* Mileševa, Serbia. Wall painting; the *Betrayal*; c. 1235.

ПРЕДАНІЕ ГНЕ

ІС ХС

34 *(above)* Sopoćani, Serbia. Wall painting; the *Dormition of the Virgin*; c. 1265.

35 *(below)* Sopoćani, Serbia. Wall painting; *Christ among the Doctors*; c. 1265.

36, 37, 38 Sopoćani, Serbia. Wall paintings; c. 1265.
(left) Christ's Appearance to the Apostles in the
Closed Room; (right) Christ's Appearance to the
Maries in the Garden; (below) Saints in the apse.

39 (*above*) Sopoćani, Serbia. Wall painting; *Death of Stephen Nemanja*; c. 1265.

40 (*below*) Sopoćani, Serbia, painting in the Prothesis; the *Annunciation*; late thirteenth century.

41 *(above)* Sopoćani, Serbia. Wall painting; detail of the *Nativity*; c. 1265.

42 *(below)* Gradać. Wall painting; detail of the *Nativity*; later thirteenth century.

43 *(above)* Peć. Church of the Holy Apostles. Painting in the apse; c. 1250

44 *(opposite above)* Arilje. Wall painting; the *Birth of the Virgin*; 1296.

45 *(opposite below)* Studenica, Serbia. Wall painting in the church of Nemanja; the *Crucifixion*; 1208.

46 *(above)* Sopoćani, Serbia. Wall painting; detail of the *Nativity*; c. 1165.

47, 48 Geraki, Greece. Wall paintings; end of the thirteenth century. *(right, above)* The *Archangel Michael*; (left) a *Bishop*.

49 Studenica, Serbia. Church of Nemanja; detail of Christ from the scene of the *Crucifixion*; 1208.

50 Panel painting in the church of Santa Maria delli Angeli, Assisi, by Giunta Pisano; detail of the crucifix.

51, 52 *(overleaf)* Boiana, Bulgaria. Wall paintings; 1295. The *Donor portraits* – (left) *The Princess Dessislava*; (right) *The Despot Kaloyan*.

53 Boiana, Bulgaria. Wall painting;
Christ Euergetes; 1259.

54 Boiana, Bulgaria. Wall painting;
Christ Teaching in the Temple; 1259.

3

Byzantium and the West in the Twelfth and Thirteenth Centuries

It sometimes happens that progressive developments in art in one field run closely parallel with those in another, even though there are apparently no very obvious links to bind the two together. Although it cannot be pretended that artistic developments in Italy were very progressive in the twelfth century, in the western world, north of the Alps, changes were taking place at this time which were even more remarkable than those which we have traced in the Byzantine area, and they are illustrated for us in a very much more complete and more continuous series of artistic monuments; in addition, the changes in the visual arts were paralleled in the west by much more progressive movements in thought and in literature than in the east. In art the development was most marked with regard to sculpture, and changes came about with most surprising rapidity. Sculptures produced at Toulouse and Moissac around 1090 are thus formal, static, severe, and show little advance upon the ivories executed by Carolingian masters more than two centuries before; yet within twenty-five years or even less, the fully fledged Romanesque style which we know from the south porch at Moissac or the tympana at such places as Autun and Vezelay, or the capitals there and at Poitiers, had been developed, and a formal, essentially static style had ceded place to one characterised above anything else by its dynamic brilliance and its profound power of expression. Within another twenty years again – if a date around 1145 may be accepted for the west doors of Chartres – this style had been once more transformed into one where naturalism was well developed: abstraction had been forsaken for realism, expression for depiction, as the figure of Christ in the tympanum of the west door there serves to show, and even if the linear treatment of the costumes and the exaggerated elongation of the column figures still indicate a considerable degree of stylisation, the faces and the small figures in subsidiary positions are tremendously fresh and alive. From this point, that of the Christ in the tympanum of the central door at Chartres or that of some of the smaller figures in the ornamental work below, the step towards the personal, three-dimensional, wholly representational sculptures of the north and south doors there, done some sixty years later, was comparatively simple, if not indeed obvious. When it had been taken, the new art we know as Gothic – humanist, rational and logical – had been born, and though it was in many respects still a medieval art, it reflected none the less the change from the age of faith to the age of reason which was taking place in the sphere of thought at exactly the same time, for it was then that the scholastics were teaching, then that learning was beginning to assume a new secular character, and then that the first universities were being founded, to take the place of the purely monastic teaching which had hitherto dominated the scene. But the change had begun in the monasteries too, if only in the creation of great libraries; as a text quoted by Haskins puts it, a monastery without a library at this time was like a castle without an armoury.

These new developments in the west were primarily a French phenomenon, and it was there that the greatest thinkers of the age were concentrated, with St Bernard of Clairvaux (1091–1153), Abbot Suger of St Denis (c. 1081–1151) and Abelard of Paris (1079–1142) foremost among them. All were more or less equally influential, though they were markedly diverse in character. St Bernard, severe in outlook, austere in belief, was wholly opposed to the great sculptured and painted decorations which for us constitute the principal glory of the age; yet he was a great leader in religious thought at a time when religion was still the most powerful influence behind thought and art. Suger, less dominant in the religious sphere, led the age in the more practical aspects of managerial efficiency and became one of the great innovator patrons of art of all time. Abelard, difficult and angular, with a permanent chip on his shoulder, led thought into new channels of a wholly creative character. The outlook of these men was wholly and completely western, and one cannot say that any of them owed any obvious debt to Byzantium. Yet the eastern world did exercise a certain degree of influence, for there are many Byzantine elements in western art of the time, to be seen in the drapery or modelling of some of the sculptures, in many of the motifs of decoration, in the basic character of some of the paintings, like those at Berzé-la-Ville or le Puy, and in the very essence of such a fresco as that depicting St Paul in St Anselm's chapel at Canterbury. Indeed Koehler even goes so far as to say that two revolutionary ideas in art, those of the articulated body and the animated figure, were carried by the crest of the Byzantine tidal wave to northern France, where a great creative genius made them the cornerstones of the new Gothic style[1]. But even if this be accepted, Romanesque and Gothic art in France remain essentially indigenous and independent styles, and the Byzantine elements must be counted as subsidiary; the art might not have been quite the same without them, but it would still have existed.

In Germany developments in art moved at a much slower pace; indeed the old Ottonian style in architecture survived with but little change right down to the thirteenth century, while in sculpture, apart from the precocious innovations of Bishop Bernward of Hildesheim early in the eleventh century, there was no activity to compare with that in France. In northern Italy the situation was more promising, for though no very rapid developments in the spheres of thought and learning took place, paintings and more especially sculptures of real artistic importance were beginning to be produced; most important were those executed by one Wiligelmo at Modena around 1099. But it was mainly in the monastic circles that culture was centred, for there were no other patrons of consequence north of Rome and no great thinkers till St Francis appeared on the scene around 1200. Government was unstable, the central parts of Italy had long been involved in continual disputes between the Germanic kings and the popes, while quite a number of cities in the north were setting themselves up as republics and strife and dissension prevailed among the merchant guilds throughout the greater part of the century.

In the papal state of Rome, on the other hand, patronage was more active, and even if less was done than in the progressive ninth century, quite a number of church decorations had been set in hand at this time, both in paint and mosaic; but there was nothing in the way of sculpture to compare with what was being produced in the north. The wall paintings were in the main wholly Romanesque in style. Those in the SS Quatri Coronati, done around 1246, are typical[2]. Some mosaics in the couch of the apse of Santa Maria in Trastevere produced between 1139 and 1143 illustrate an earlier trend (Plate 68). They depict Christ and the Virgin enthroned, with St Callixtus, St Lawrence and the donor, Julius by name, to the right, and St Peter, St Cornelius and an individual named Katopodius to the left. As in most of the work done in Italy at this time the style is hard and rigid, and though it is basically Byzantine, there are no hints whatsoever of the humanistic, expressive manner that characterises the Revival style which was already to the fore in progressive monuments in the Byzantine world. Any elements here and elsewhere in Italy that are to be traced to Byzantium owe a debt either to the influences of the monumental art of the Second Golden Age (843 – c. 1100), or were inherited from Early Christian sources which left a legacy to Italy and to the Byzantine world alike. This heritage was often important, as for example in the paintings in San Pietro at Ferentillo in the hills above Terni, executed probably during the last quarter of the twelfth century. They have a marked classical character, and the scene of Adam naming the animals seems to have a direct relationship with the title page of the Godescalco Gospels, in spite of the difference of the actual theme. The style of these paintings, with their naturalistic approach and their interest in the picturesque, is quite distinct from that of the more or less contemporary *Virgin and Child between Santa Pudenziana and Santa Praxede* in Santa Praxede in Rome. There the manner is Byzantine, though the work is rigid and dry and shows no hints of the liveliness of the Revival.

Further to the south, the influence of the contemporary Byzantine world had been important in the eleventh century, for Abbot Desiderius (Abbot 1058–86) had introduced Byzantine workmen at Montecassino. The paintings that were executed by them have perished, but those in the church of San Angelo in Formis at Capua are generally taken as typical of the style that resulted, though they are not all of the time of Desiderius. But it is a great mistake to regard this work as almost wholly Byzantine, as certain writers, who are not familiar with Byzantine art, sometimes tend to do. It represents, in truth, a very hybrid style, more Romanesque than Byzantine, as a comparison of the paintings in the church with those in the porch, added in the second half of the twelfth century, serves to show[3]. The work in the porch must have been done by a Greek, probably from Constantinople; that in the church must have been by Italians whose style was mainly western even if they had assimilated a good many Byzantine elements, more especially with regard to iconography and the rendering of details such as thrones, architecture or costumes.

In a similar way Greek masters worked roughly a century later for the Sicilian kings, but their style remained pure and was but little adulterated even when the work was done not by immigrant Greeks but by Sicilians whom the Greeks had taught. Most of these men had, however, been schooled in the monumental, conservative style of mid-Byzantine art, and it was really only in the last of the great Sicilian decorations, that at Monreale, that the dynamism of the Revival style began to make itself felt. Even so, the mosaics of Monreale lacked much of the excellence of the best Byzantine work and, as we have seen, they are more closely related to a provincial decoration like that of Kurbinovo than to a metropolitan one like Nerez (see p. 35)[4].

This brief summary suggests that till the later years of the twelfth century art in Italy on the whole showed less sign of vitality than that of France and though good sculptures were done there, as at Modena, there was little to equal the glories of the west door of Chartres, while in painting Italian work lacked both the energy of the French and the polished elegance of the Byzantine Revival. It remained on the whole sterile and unproductive, showing little indication of the change that was in the air both in the east and to the north of the alps. The real question at issue, as far as Italy is concerned, is thus what happened there in the later twelfth and earlier thirteenth centuries, rather than what happened at an earlier date. How far did Romanesque art develop on its own? When did the spirit of humanism and dynamism begin to appear? How far did contacts with the Byzantine world, made either in the later twelfth century or at the beginning of the thirteenth as a result of the Latin conquest of Constantinople in 1204, bring about a change?

In his study of art in Italy in the thirteenth century Van Marle distinguished three main groups or families. One is determined primarily on the basis of form and subject matter; it is made up of the painted crosses bearing the crucified Christ as their main decoration; his second is a provincial one and comprises only works of very secondary quality; his third he terms the Byzantinising. The second group may be dismissed first, for it is the one that concerns us least. The majority of the painters to be included in it worked in a rather primitive, didactic style and it cannot be pretended that their paintings are of great artistic significance, with the exception perhaps of the works of a few more outstanding men such as Berlinghiero and Bonaventura Berlinghieri, who worked at Lucca from about 1215 to 1240 and 1228 to 1274 respectively. In the work of all of the men who may be assigned to this group, Byzantine elements are present, but they are all of a conservative character, and could even have been assimilated at the time that Greek craftsmen were introduced by Abbot Desiderius. There is nothing to indicate that work of the progressive character of Nerez, still less that of the contemporary metropolitan school, as we see it at Mileševa, Sopoćani or Trebizond, had any effect on them whatsoever.

Paintings of Van Marle's first group, the painted crosses, are from our point of view more interesting. Most of them were produced in the region of Pisa. The earliest would appear to be a cross at Sarzana, which has been dated to 1138[5]. Christ is depicted as still alive, with eyes fully open; the drawing is wooden and rigid, and there is little attempt to convey the agony and emotion of the scene. The same is true of most of the twelfth or even the earlier thirteenth-century examples in Italy. In this respect they are a long way behind the wall paintings of the Crucifixion at Studenica and Žiča in Yugoslavia, the former dated to 1208, where Christ is shown as already dead, with closed eyes, and where the scene is rendered with considerable expression (see pp. 46 f.). It would thus seem that the rendering of the scene where the conception of the pathetic was to the fore had been developed to a more marked degree in the Byzantine world than was the case in Italy. But the question of style must also be considered here, for the Studenica and Žiča frescoes stand apart from other paintings of the age in the Byzantine world and show a distinct relationship with the work of Giunta Pisano. Were they the product of a local craftsman whose style heralded that of the Pisani, or was a Pisan painter working in Yugoslavia at a date earlier than that of any paintings of the type that we know in Italy? The question must for the moment remain open[6]. What is sure is that the development of the pathetic, humanistic version of the Crucifixion theme seems to have progressed further in the Byzantine world than in the Italian sphere. In view of the developments towards humanism made at Nerez by 1164, and in the icon of *Our Lady of Vladimir* as early as about 1130, this is perhaps not surprising.

Van Marle terms his third group the Byzantinising. Most writers agree in noting

its existence, but there is dispute as to what paintings should be assigned to it, and there is little uniformity as to what precisely is implied by the term Byzantine. Often it is used to describe works which are rigid and severe through the incompetence of the artist rather than because of any real influence from Byzantium or any avowed intention to follow a formalistic trend. At other times the term is employed to describe works of a conservative character in which the same Early Christian elements are apparent as those to be seen in truly Byzantine products, though the similarities are due to what both may have inherited from a common ancestor rather than to any contemporary links. At times it serves to describe works which show the influence of the polished metropolitan style of Constantinople; at others the more dramatic art that originally stemmed from Syria and was subsequently developed in monastic centres in the east is envisaged. Indeed, de Francovich has even gone so far as to explain the spirited character of the Monreale mosaics as the result of a survival of the Syrian style as we see it at the outset in such a manuscript as the Sinope codex in the Bibliothèque Nationale[7]. Elements that stemmed ultimately from Syria certainly exercised an influence on the development of Byzantine art in early times, and they were no doubt influential in Italy too, but by the eleventh century they had become so much a part of the complex pattern of Mediterranean art as a whole that it is hardly possible to attribute stylistic characteristics to Syria alone. One can, however, distinguish the more dramatic style which is usually termed the monastic from the more elegant and polished one which was associated with the capital. In view of this confusion it is essential to clarify what exactly we imply by the term Byzantine before we proceed with the enquiry.

That there was a marked degree of Byzantine influence in Italy at this time is not to be disputed – the general acceptance of the term *Maniera Greca* used so freely by Vasari is proof of it. What is important from our point of view is to distinguish the influences exercised by contemporary Byzantine art from those which survived from earlier times, with the object of determining which of the elements that were new in the art of the thirteenth century in Italy should be regarded as indigenous and which were taken over from the progressive art of the Byzantine world, having first been developed there as features of our Revival style. Work in the so-called *Maniera Greca* was no doubt dead and second-rate, and deserved all the condemnation that Vasari cast upon it, but the Revival manner as we see it at Mileševa and elsewhere was something very different. How far were developments in Italy indebted to this trend?

The most outstanding works on Italian soil in which the penetration of the Revival style is involved are probably the frescoes in the crypt of the Cathedral at Aquilea, which have recently formed the theme of a study by Mademoiselle Valland[8]. Their date has been disputed, but Mlle Valland's attribution to a date soon after 1200 can hardly be disputed. She regards the paintings as expressing the spirit of the budding Renaissance rather than as monuments of the old medieval art. True, there are elements in their make-up that are essentially Romanesque, but taken as a whole they belong to a progressive trend, which can only be described as the result of the penetration of the Revival style into the western world. Their style is thus not far removed from that of the paintings at Mileševa, and they are clearly to be regarded as a manifestation of the same movement in art. If those authorities are correct who assign them to a date earlier than that of the paintings at Mileševa, this can only be explained if we accept the existence of an earlier prototype common to both, which has now disappeared. It was, no doubt, to be found in Constantinople.

XIII Sopoćani, Serbia. Wall painting in the apse; *Saints*; c. 1265

81

In addition to scenes from the lives of the two patron saints of the church, St Hermagouras and St Fortunatus, four subjects from the New Testament decorated the Aquilea crypt – the *Crucifixion*, the *Deposition*, the *Lamentation* and the *Dormition of the Virgin* (Plates 69 and 70) – all be it noted scenes of an emotional character where sadness dominates, and all scenes where the Virgin, emblem of human compassion and suffering, has a prominent role to play. All follow ultimate Byzantine prototypes, and all show an increasing interest in the rendering of human emotions and suggest that the painter had paid close attention to the actual observation of life. In the *Crucifixion*, for example, the arrangement is basically Byzantine, but the old system of hierarchy, where the more important figures are considerably larger than the others, so clearly to the fore in the scene of the Maries at the Sepulchre at Mileševa, has been forsaken – a significant indication of the stress on humanism. The rendering may be contrasted with the more conservative manner that characterises the depiction of this scene in the mosaics of St Mark's at Venice (Plate 71), where Christ is half as tall again as the Virgin and St John and nearly double the size of Longinus and Stephaton. The comparison also illustrates the greater stress laid on emotion in the Aquilea painting, as well as the tender subtlety of the treatment of Christ; he is conceived as a suffering human, not as a symbol of divine power.

The rendering of the *Deposition* at Aquilea is again distinctive, for the Virgin holds Christ's body and weeps over it: a sort of Lamentation before its time, as Miss Valland describes it (Plate 70). The depiction of the scene has thus developed quite considerably since the time of Nerez, but is very close indeed to that at Mileševa done around 1235. The same scheme was reproduced from fifty to a hundred years later by numerous painters in Italy. The scene of the Lamentation itself again follows Nerez and is paralleled at Mileševa; the same model must have served at an even earlier date for a painting in the church of St Neophytos at Paphos in Cyprus dated to about 1183([9]). In Italy the theme was only adopted in the later thirteenth century, and it did not become general till the fourteenth.

The inclusion of the *Dormition of the Virgin* in a decoration restricted to no more than four subjects is perhaps even more significant with regard to the problem of influences and origins, for it was a scene that was still very unusual in the west, whereas it had been normal in Byzantine iconography at least since the eleventh century; indeed its presence at Aquilea is a stronger pointer to the basically Byzantine character of this decoration than any other single factor, while the fundamentally abstract treatment of the composition is also part of the legacy that Byzantium was to hand on to the art of Italy in the thirteenth century, and through it to that of the Renaissance. And it may again be stressed that it is not the sterile, provincial and essentially conservative style which is generally referred to as the *Maniera Greca* that concerns us here, but rather a progressive, humanist and accomplished art, in which innovations of the first importance were already taking place. Hints of the style are to be seen again in a fresco of the Crucifixion at Salerno([10]), and future discoveries may disclose that other works of the same character existed elsewhere on Italian soil, for there is every reason to believe that such works exercised a considerable influence on the more progressive artists of the thirteenth century, even on the really great men like Cavallini and Cimabue.

Cavallini was working from about 1270 till 1308, but the earliest of his productions that have come down to us are mosaics in the apse of Santa Maria in Trastevere at Rome (Plate 68). They are made up of a number of panels in square frames depicting six of the great feasts of the church, namely the *Birth of the Virgin*, the *Annunciation*, the *Nativity*, the *Adoration*, the *Presentation* and the *Dormition*; in the centre is a medallion enclosing the Virgin and Child with St Paul on one side and St Peter and the donor, Bertoldo, on the other[11]. This was probably done in 1291; some of the other panels may be a little later. There are certain western features, such as the nature of the costumes, the character of the magi, and the naturalism of the rocks in the *Adoration*, but in general both iconography and style are very markedly Byzantine. The debt here is perhaps to be attributed to Byzantine art of the monumental trend rather than to that of the Revival, but in much of his work Cavallini's approach was very closely akin to that made by the anonymous masters who worked at Mileševa, Sopoćani or Trebizond.

The famous fresco of the *Last Judgement* in Santa Cecilia at Rome, done probably in 1293, shows the imprint of Cavallini's personality very much more clearly than the mosaic (Plate 72), but there are also elements that suggest relationships with progressive Byzantine painting like that in Hagia Sophia at Trebizond. For example, the archangels are clothed in Byzantine imperial costume and their wings are done in a way that is wellnigh identical with those at Trebizond, the highlights are applied in a similar fashion, and the faces are modelled on the same type of *terra verde* undercoat, the lighter colours being applied last, as was usual in Byzantine painting. The colouring in general savours of the system developed in work of the Byzantine Revival, and often the light seems to come from some inner source rather than to have been cast naturally, a feature which was to become progressively more important as Byzantine painting developed.

The array of apostles in Santa Cecilia suggests at once a comparison with the similar figures in the famous *Last Judgement* at Vladimir, a work of the Revival, though it dates from as early as 1193. Only the mitres of the Bishops and the more naturalistic treatment of certain figures, like the sleeping Jacob, fall into the sphere of western rather than Byzantine art. Apart from this, Cavallini's personal style was well developed; the faces show great individuality and they, rather than the iconography, the composition, or the colouring, stamp the Santa Cecilia fresco as an Italian rather than a Byzantine product. A return to Roman models of the classical period has been suggested in connection with Cavallini's work, but this seems unlikely. Rather are we in the presence here of a monument in the manner of the Byzantine Revival, though it is one very deeply imbued with the personal style of a great individual artist.

Cavallini's art as we see it in the Santa Cecilia frescoes is thus both sympathetic and progressive. That of Cimabue (*c.* 1240–1302), his Florentine contemporary, was perhaps more monumental, but it was at the same time a good deal less personal; and it was indeed at the same time more conservative, for the Byzantine elements we see here often belong to the monumental rather than to the Revival style. It is quite wrong to accept the popular belief that it was only in Florence that forward looking art could be produced, and it would indeed be juster to say that by the last quarter of the thirteenth century art in Florence represents for us the end of an old style in Italy rather than the birth of a new one, even if it was there that the dividing line was most clearly marked between the Italian art of the thirteenth century and the style which was to blossom in the fourteenth, under Giotto's influence, as something wholly new.

This new art first saw the light in sculpture at the hands of such men as Nicola Pisano (*c.* 1220–78), his son Giovanni (*c.* 1245–1314), or Arnolfo di Cambio (*c.* 1245–1302). Nicola's wholly revolutionary pulpit for Pisa was finished in 1260, and it is there that we see for the first time a profound concern with the real and the material, and it is this that distinguishes the new Italian art from the Revival style in Byzantium. Nicola, and Arnolfo with him, were not content with the concentration on the spiritual which was so much to the fore in the Byzantine sphere. They sought the actual, and in this respect Giotto was their direct disciple(¹²). There was little of the old mystic, spiritual approach of the Byzantines in his art, nor did it reflect very much of the ascetic outlook of St Francis of Assisi, though Giotto was closely concerned with the development of the St Francis iconographical cycle at Assisi. In fact he stood apart, owing a debt to Byzantium as regards iconography, but not in the basic character of his art, and developing ideas which were as new as those of St Francis, but which ran along a wholly distinct course.

It was to be a long time before the rest of Italy caught up with Giotto's progress. What Offner defines as the stark statement, the heroic system and the obvious intellectualism of Giotto's art was far from being a universal law in Italy even as late as the mid-fourteenth century. As he says, 'Giotto's art, by idealising action and psychology . . . . . . arrested the mobility of life and burdened the sensibilities by its monumental weight'(¹³). The Byzantines who worked at almost exactly the same moment at Kariye Camii in Constantinople were not impelled by such weighty aims; they sought beauty, life, humanism, but in a gayer, lighter vein, and they were not intimately concerned with the deeper emotions of the world or even with the affairs of eternity; rather their aim was to recount the Bible story so that it was comprehensible to men of the material world and yet remained in itself a thing of the spirit. And so, if we accept Offner's thesis, did certain of the trecento painters of Italy. Like their Byzantine contemporaries, they avoided the dramatic and sought to depict the themes of Our Lord's life simply, with delicacy and with tenderness. Pucino di Bonaghida's *Crucifixion*, with an illustration of which Offner opens his study, is wholly and completely in this vein. But neither he nor any other of these Italians, with the exception of Duccio, were as consummate artists as was the Byzantine master who worked at Kariye Camii, and from the purely artistic point of view the work of the general run of painters in Italy around 1300 was not up to the standard of the best that was done at the same date by a whole series of anonymous Byzantines.

Though in his search for realism, in his sculpturesque, three-dimensional approach, and in the interest he took in the material world around him, Giotto was cutting wholly new ground, he nevertheless owed a considerable debt to earlier models, both with regard to iconography and at times with regard to style also, and those models were in many cases Byzantine and belonged to the Revival trend of art as we see it at Mileševa and Sopoćani, and not to the desiccated provincial style of Italy, or even to the monumental style of the great middle period of Byzantine art as we see it at Daphni. This debt is clearly to be observed if we study the paintings of the Arena Chapel at Padua, where work began about 1303. There the arrangement of the *Nativity*, the *Baptism*, the *Presentation in the Temple*, the *Flight into Egypt*, the *Raising of Lazarus*, the *Entry into Jerusalem*, the *Betrayal*, the *Crucifixion* and the *Lamentation* all follow Byzantine prototypes closely (Plate 73), while details of many other scenes must also unquestionably have been derived from Byzantine or early Christian models. Variations of the theme of the curtains knotted round a pillar which we see in the *Annunciation* thus reappear time and again in Christian art throughout Europe; the curious, almost geometric rocks follow the same convention as in much early Byzantine art, though there they are less solid, more two-dimensional; the massive, sculpturesque figures who kneel before our Lord in the *Raising of Lazarus* or beside the body in the *Lamentat-*

58 *(below)* Ivanovo, Bulgaria. The
Anastasis; second half thirteenth century.

57 *(left and opposite above)* Trebizond, Church of Hagia Sophia. Wall painting in the dome; *choir of angels*; c. 1260.

59 Sofia, the Church of St George. Wall painting; early fourteenth century.

60 *(below)* Trebizond, Church of Hagia Sophia. Wall painting; the *Appearance of Christ on the Shores of Lake Tiberias*; c. 1260.

61 Trebizond, Church of Hagia Sophia. Wall paintings in the pendentives of the dome; the *Anastasis* and the *Baptism*.

63, 64 Trebizond, Church of Hagia Sophia. Wall painting; c. 1260. The *Feeding of the Five Thousand* — *(opposite above)* north end of narthex — *(opposite below)* west vault of narthex.

62 *(below)* Trebizond, Church of Hagia Sophia. Wall painting; the *Marriage Feast at Cana*; c. 1260.

65, 66 Trebizond, Church of Hagia Sophia. Wall paintings; c. 1260; (above) head of angel in *Jacob's Struggle*; (below) head of *St Bartholomew*.

67 Panel painting; the *Virgin and Child*; late thirteenth century. The National Gallery of Art, Washington.

68 *(overleaf)* Rome, Santa Maria in Trastevere. Mosaic in the apse; *(above) Christ and the Virgin enthroned*, and *(below)* scenes by Cavallini.

MARCVS   MATHEVS

ECCEVIRGOCONCI
PIETETPARIETFILIVM

ISAIAS·PPHA

IOHS   LVCAS

HIEREMIAS PPH

69 (opposite above) Aquilea Cathedral. Wall paintings in the crypt; the *Crucifixion*; first half of thirteenth century.

70 (opposite below) Aquilea Cathedral. Wall paintings in the crypt; the *Deposition*; first half of thirteenth century.

71 (right) St Mark's, Venice. Mosaic; the *Crucifixion*; twelfth century.

72 (below) Rome, Santa Cecilia. Detail of wall painting of the *Last Judgement* by Pietro Cavallini; end of thirteenth century.

73, 74 Padua, the Arena Chapel. Wall paintings by Giotto; c. 1303; *(above)* the *Lamentation*; *(below)* the *Last Supper*.

75, 76 The Maestà, Siena, by Duccio; early fourteenth century. *(above)* The *Washing of the Feet*; *(below)* the *Betrayal*.

77 Mount Athos, Karyes, Church of the Protaton. Wall painting;
the *Washing of the Feet*; c. 1300.

78 *(below)* Mount Athos, Karyes, Church of the Protaton. Wall painting; *the Baptism*;
c. 1300.

79 Salonica, Chapel of St Euthemios in the Church of St Demetrios.
The *Communion of the Apostles*; early fourteenth century.

80 *(below)* Mount Athos, Karyes, Church of the Protaton. Detail from the
scene of the *Baptism*; c. 1300.

ion, are to be found a century earlier at Mileševa and again at Sopoćani in Yugo-slavia. The kneeling figures of the Maries at Sopoćani when Christ appears before them in the garden (Plate 37), were for instance reproduced wellnigh exactly by Giotto in the *Lamentation* at Padua, which is clearly a late link in a chain which began at Nerez and continued elsewhere in Yugoslavia and at Aquilea. But the feeling, the rendering of the faces and the interest in massive, three-dimensional form, were more fully developed by Giotto, and in the arrangement of many of his scenes he adopted entirely new systems in which he sought to free art from the old Byzantine abstraction. In the *Last Supper*, for example, Giotto attempted the daring experiment of placing five of the apostles with their backs to the spectator (Plate 74), in opposition to the Byzantine system of ranging all facing the observer behind the curve of a D-shaped table, with the straight side unoccupied. Giotto's experiment was extremely venturesome, but it must also be admitted that with regard to this scene it was not wholly successful and the ways in which the five apostles gaze into their soup-plate-like haloes is somewhat grotesque.

In Siena, where the old aristocracy played a more important role in dictating the outlook, a widespread demand for high quality was allied with a greater con-servatism of taste, and the fact that the Sienese were Ghibellines whereas the Florentines were of the Guelph persuasion helped to accentuate the differences of outlook. No doubt it was the aristocratic nature of the patronage which was respon-sible for the very Byzantine character of the art, especially that of Duccio (*c.* 1250–1319) as exemplified in the scenes on the back of his *Maestà*, done around 1311. It is virtually an iconostasis in miniature, while the Madonna on the obverse was a direct descendant of the Madonnas of Byzantium, savouring of the spiritual world rather than of the human; it contrasts markedly with Giotto's rendering of the same theme now in the Uffizi at Florence, which is far more forceful, far more worldly. And a Madonna and Child done by Guido da Siena in 1262 belongs equally to the Byzantine tradition; it may be described as a Sienese interpretation of the Byzantine *Hodegetria*. The new freedom that characterises the treatment of the child's legs — they are crossed — attests once again the fact that any debt to Byzantium was owed, not to the monumental art of the middle period or to the dry *Maniera Greca*, but to the progressive Revival style of the twelfth and thir-teenth centuries[14].

It is, however, in the treatment of the scenes on the back of the *Maestà* that Duccio's debt to the art of the Byzantine Revival is most clearly illustrated. There his jewel-like colours and wholly unworldly approach are quite distinctive. With regard to detail, the most striking comparison between his work and the Byzantine is in the scene of the *Betrayal*, for the poses adopted by Duccio are almost identical with those followed at Mileševa (Plate 76). Duccio's rendering of the *Washing of the Feet* is closely parallel to that in the Protaton on Athos (*c.* 1300) (Plates 75 and 77), as is his *Entry into Jerusalem* to that at Vatoperi (1312). Such instances could be multiplied[15], and are such as to indicate that they are not to be attributed to the survival of elements from some prototype common to Duccio and to the Byzan-tines alike, but are due rather to contemporary contacts. Could Duccio have gone to Constantinople? It is certainly a possibility. Or he may have seen in Italy Byzantine miniatures or panels like the lovely little icon of St Michael now in the Pisa gallery. Such works, as Lazarev has shown[16], had already begun to exercise a considerable influence in Siena even before the turn of the century. It was to these later Byzantine panels that Duccio was indebted for his exquisite rhythms, for the elegant proportions of his figures, for their easy movements, for the elaborate

81 *(opposite)* Mount Athos, Monastery of Chilandari. Wall painting; the *Raising of Lazarus*; c. 1302.

nature of the landscape and architectural backgrounds, for his generally advanced conception of space, and for the profoundly spiritual character of his work.

Madonna panels done by Coppo di Marcovaldo and Guido da Siena show hints of the same manner. In spite of the way in which the Virgin holds the Child's toe in that by Coppo di Marcovaldo of 1261 in Santa Maria dei Servi at Siena, the character is Byzantine, and though his rather similar Madonna in the church of the same designation at Orvieto is marked at once as Italian by the crown on the Virgin's head, it too has the character of an icon[17]. Again it is often hard to say whether many of the panels produced in Venice in the course of the thirteenth and fourteenth centuries are to be classed as icons or as western panels, for Byzantine elements are to the fore in much of the work produced there, including that of the most outstanding of the Venetian painters at the time, Paolo Veneziano (1333–62)[18]. These Venetian works were, however, inspired not so much by the thirteenth-century Revival style as we see it at Mileševa, Sopoćani or Trebizond, but rather by the developed Palaeologan art of the fourteenth century, and they are thus distinct in character from the work of Cimabue, Cavallini or Giotto. The work of these men represents the end of a tradition. Thereafter the links with the Byzantine world were to a great extent severed in central Italy, but in Venice they were maintained till the Turkish conquest of Constantinople in 1453; and even after that date they continued, for there was an influential Greek Orthodox colony in Venice. In the fourteenth and fifteenth centuries Venetian art was thus conservative.

In Florence the brilliant future of the Italian Renaissance, pagan in spirit, experimental in approach, lay ahead. In the Byzantine world Palaeologan art was to follow a less adventurous course essentially spiritual and Christian in character, but it was none the less capable of producing great works, as the wall paintings of Mistra or panels like the *Virgin of Pimen* done in Constantinople late in the fourteenth century, serve to prove (Plate 126). But for a brief period, in the twelfth and thirteenth centuries, the Byzantine world led the van and Italy followed in her wake, and if for no other reason than this, the story of Byzantine painting in these years must be just as significant to students of western culture as to Byzantine specialists. And to those who love fine works for their own sake, the mosaics of Kariye or the fourteenth-century icons of Byzantium and Russia stand as a lasting glory, no less worthy representatives of the eastern trend than Giotto's paintings in the Arena chapel are worthy of the western.

4

The Macedonian School in the Later Thirteenth and Fourteenth Centuries

When the study of later Byzantine painting first began in the earlier years of this century, the great French scholar Gabriel Millet recognised the existence of two major schools which he termed respectively the Macedonian and the Cretan. He based his distinction primarily on iconographical evidence – the former showing closer links with Syrian, the latter with Constantinopolitan prototypes, though there were certain factors of style that served to separate them also, notably a love of elegance and a taste for the inclusion of decorative elements in the Cretan and a search for realism and drama in the Macedonian. Though Millet's conclusions regarding the nature and development of the Cretan school can now hardly be accepted, his Macedonian school still stands as an entity[1]. It is characterised by a dramatic approach, as well as by a deep, rather heavy colouring, where the 'inner light' (see pp. 165 and 181), so important in later metropolitan and much Russian painting, is absent. Disputes have, however, arisen as to the origins of this school, and our study of it must begin by calling attention to a controversy. On the one hand, many authorities, especially the Greek scholars, maintain that this style, which flourished in Macedonia and much of Greece from the end of the thirteenth century onwards, had its birth in Salonica. Its dissemination was due, they maintain, to the influence of painters who had been trained and worked in what was then and had for a long time been the second city of the Byzantine world; virtually all the painters of consequence who were associated with the school in any case till about 1330, were, they think, of Greek nationality. On the other hand, many others, with Yugoslav authorities foremost among them, hold that most of the painters worked as itinerant artists, having no particular centre, and many of them, they think, were Slavs; the characteristics of what may be called the Macedonian school, according to this view, were developed in the main as the direct result of the Slav nationality of the painters. For them the role of Salonica was much more limited than the Greeks believe, even though it must be accepted that the influence of a great city would undoubtedly have been considerable.

Before attempting to reach any final conclusion on this matter it is essential to look carefully at the monuments themselves. Let us therefore begin with those in Salonica itself.

Some rather fragmentary paintings in the narthex of the Church of the Virgin of the Coppersmiths are the earliest that survive[2]; they are probably to be assigned to the eleventh century, and so fall outside the scope of this survey. They are however vigorous and dramatic and if they wholly lack the sophisticated grandeur of typical thirteenth century work like that at Mileševa and Sopoćani, they nevertheless herald the style of the fully-fledged Macedonian school, as we see it developed in the Protaton on Mount Athos done around 1300. Paintings in the chapel of St Euthemios in the basilica of St Demetrius, are the next with regard to date – they were done in 1303. One of them, the scene of the *Communion of the Apostles* (Plate 79), was reproduced in colour by Professor Sotiriou in his large book on St Demetrius; the plate shows more than can be seen on the spot today[3]. The colouring would appear to have been comparatively bright, with a marked preponderance of blue; that of the paintings in the church of the Virgin of the Coppersmiths was more sombre. In both series of paintings however the scenes are rendered with vividness and expression; there is a great sense of movement, the attitudes are rather angular, the figures squat rather than elegant, the heads small but expressive. In this respect they contrast with those in the mosaics in the dome and on the vaults of the church of the Holy Apostles at Salonica, which date from 1312 (see p. 151). The style of the mosaics is much closer to that of the work in Kariye Camii at Constantinople and it is hard to accept the conclusions of Xyngopoulos, who sees in the mosaics of the Holy Apostles marked traces of the tendency towards the dramatic which characterises the Macedonian School. Rather would they seem to represent a minor variant of the Constantinopolitan style of the fourteenth century.

The paintings in the chapel of St Euthemios have recently been compared by Xyngopoulos to those in the Protaton at Karyes on Mount Athos. These were at one time regarded as sixteenth-century works because of an associated inscription which mentions the date 1540. The majority of them had certainly undergone a good deal of restoration at this time, but even in their restored condition, the earlier paintings survived in places untouched, as in a lovely depiction of the Virgin appearing to St Pachomios[4], while the iconography and composition were but little affected by the restoration, even if certain details were altered. The paintings have now been cleaned and Xyngopoulos makes out a very good case for believing that all of them belong to the original decoration of the church, done under the patronage of Andronicos Palaeologos (1282–1328) early in the fourteenth century. The work is both very individual and very dramatic. The heads are curiously foreshortened, the poses angular and dynamic, the colours brilliant – much more so even than in the Chapel of St Euthemios at Salonica. The painter may have been trained in the same school, but he was certainly a different individual from the man who worked at Salonica and he was possessed of a very personal style of his own. This is well illustrated in his rendering of the scenes of the *Washing of the Feet* (Plate 77) and the *Baptism*, which are dramatic, angular, forceful (Plate 78). Especially striking are the children who dance on a bridge in the left-hand corner of the latter (Plate 80); they are vivid and expressive and the effect is quite unlike anything that pertains to Constantinople, but the work here does resemble, as we shall see, many of the paintings produced in the early fourteenth century in Yugoslavia.

Xyngopoulos suggests that the artist who was responsible for the paintings of the Protaton was actually a man named Panseleinos, who has long been famed in the Greek world. There has however been much argument as to when he lived; some have proposed that he worked as early as the eleventh century, though they have not assigned any actual paintings to him. Prokopiou seeks to identify him with a painter who was active in Yugoslavia around 1300, who is known there as Astrapas[5]; others believe that he worked in the sixteenth century, and paintings of this date in one of the monasteries at the Meteora have been attributed to him.

Gabriel Millet regarded him as the most outstanding figure of the Macedonian school, and set him against another painter called Theophanes, the most important exponent of the Cretan school on Athos, who was responsible for the decoration of the monastery of the Lavra in 1535, and that of Stavronikita in 1546. Now that the paintings of the Protaton have been cleaned and are available for study in their original guise, there seems good reason to accept Xyngopoulos' conclusions and to regard Panseleinos as the man responsible for the original Protaton paintings done soon after 1300[6].

Any other early manifestations of this school on Athos have all been very considerably overpainted; the Catholicon or main church in the Monastery of Chilandari, painted in 1302, was restored in 1804; that at Vatopedi (1312) was redone in 1819. It would seem, however, that the original outlines of the figures were in both cases followed fairly exactly by the restorers. Revolting though the colours and the surface texture of these overpaintings are, enough nevertheless survives of the original outline to make of them important documents for iconographical study, and a few scenes from these decorations may be noted in passing. At Chilandari, for example, there is a very full cycle and a number of scenes which are not known elsewhere appear for the first time; the *Preparation of the Cross* and the *Setting of Christ's Body on the Cross* are typical not only of the tendency towards the introduction of numerous subsidiary scenes which began in the twelfth century at Nerez, but also of the angular, dynamic approach of the painters of the Macedonian school. The same style indeed characterises the depiction of the more familiar scenes like the *Raising* of *Lazarus* (Plate 81). The *Entry into Jerusalem* at Vatopedi again illustrates these features, as well as the tendency towards realism, for the scene is conceived in considerable depth. Christ's mule occupies the foreground, and the landscape opens out behind, with the figures in the distance shown on a reduced scale. The buildings are more solid and much truer to life than the strange decorative architectural fantasies which occupy the backgrounds at Kariye, though it must be remembered that some of the detail may be due to the hand of the restorer.

The monastery of Chilandari on Athos was founded by King Milutin of Serbia, also known as Stephen Uros II, whose wife was the daughter of the Byzantine Emperor Andronicos II. He was also responsible for founding a series of churches in Macedonia, and collected together a number of painters to work for him there. Three names, Astrapas, Michael and Eutychios are recorded. Most Serbian authorities, notably Radojćić, regard these as three separate individuals and hold that the name Astrapas, which is in any case a pseudonym, for it means lightning, referred either to the father or to the master of Michael[7]. All three names appear on the paintings in St Clement's at Ochrid – that of Eutychios alone and those of Astrapas and Michael together; the latter's signature appears as Χείρ Μὶχαηλ του Αδτράπα, 'the hand of Michael of Astrapas'. In the porch of the church of the Virgin at Prizren, on the other hand the signature of Astrapas appears alone, and this lends weight to Radojćić's suggestion. But Xyngopoulos argues that the word του in this case does not necessarily imply any separate identity, but is like the 'de' in a French name, and he insists that Astrapas and Michael are one and the same person. He is followed in this by Milkovic-Pepek[8]. All agree as to the separate identity of Eutychios. The problem will perhaps only be solved finally if and when more signatures are discovered, but one thing already seems sure, namely that if some of the paintings in the body of the church at Prizren are by Astrapas as well as those in the porch, then he was most certainly a distinct individual working in a style much closer to that of Constantinople than that of either of the others.

This problem is, however, of minor significance in contrast to the arguments which have raged as to the nationality of these men and the character of the art which they produced. One group of scholars, with Xyngopoulos and Prokopiou at its head, claims them as Greeks from Salonica. Another, supported by Lazarev and most of the Yugoslav scholars, insists that they were Serbs who worked in various places under the patronage of King Milutin; they would even assign the painting of the Protaton on Athos to them([9]). According to a third view, which was put forward by the late V. R. Petković, they were to be regarded as what he termed 'Pictores Graeci', painters of Orthodox faith from the Adriatic. Though there was certainly an important group of painters in that region, there seems no reason at all to associate paintings of the type done by Michael, Eutychios and Astrapas with it, and the suggestion may be summarily dismissed; it was in any case put forward some years ago, when few frescoes in Macedonia had been cleaned and when they had been much less studied than is the case today. But both the Greek and the Serb theories are valid and both deserve close examination.

The first church in point of date where the signatures appear is that of the Virgin Perebleptos, also known as St Clement, at Ochrid, which was built in 1295. Eutychios' signature is to be found on the belt of St Procopios, that of Michael on the sword carried by St Mercury. The paintings in this church have recently been cleaned and are now very striking in appearance. The colours are brilliant, even garish, and the effect is indeed surprising in contrast to that to be experienced in most Byzantine churches of the age, where the colours tend to be rather dull and sombre. Even allowing for the effects of cleaning, it is obvious that the men who executed those at Ochrid favoured a particularly vivid and varied palette. Even in a monochrome reproduction the clear-cut, brilliant character of the work is apparent. All the subtle nuances and restrained delicacy of Constantinopolitan painting are absent, and in contrast the work seems crude and rather barbaric, while the compositions are angular and tend to be over-full. The scene of the *Betrayal* is typical; no figure is excluded, no detail omitted, and little is left to the imagination (Plate 83). Here, as also in the adjacent scene of the *Sleeping Apostles in the Garden*, considerable attention has been paid to the three-dimensional nature of the landscape. In the rendering of the *Birth of the Virgin*, at a lower level on the same wall, a similar preoccupation is apparent with regard to the architecture. In the scene of the *Dormition of the Virgin* the architecture has been used to create an impression of limitless depth with very considerable effect (Plate 84). It is a tremendously impressive and inspiring composition, even if the colours are somewhat harsh and unsympathetic.

The work of the two painters Michael and Eutychios, who were responsible for this decoration, is closely akin, but Radojčić, who has made a careful study of it, claims that that of Michael is characterised by a softer, more delicate, line and by more gentle, subtler colouring, while that of Eutychios is harsher and more dynamic and is at its best when seen from a distance. The scene of the *Dormition* is probably to be assigned to him.

Though in some of the other works of Michael and Eutychios, notably that at Staro Nagoričino, the colours are more sombre, the vividness of line and the dramatic effect of the compositions are equally clearly marked. They worked in 1307 in the church of St Nikitas at Čučer near Skopolje and in 1317–8 in the church at Staro Nagoričino; the *Mocking of Christ* there is almost as dramatic as a picture by Hogarth (Plate 82), and the scene of the *Cleansing of the Temple* in the church of

St Nikitas at Čučer is even more dramatic (Plate 85). Merchants, cattle, sheep and goats all flee before Christ, the tables are overturned, the people ashamed and embarrassed. The whole event is conceived in terms of the world around us, and this effect is intensified by the solid nature of the architecture in the background of each scene. Some paintings at Žiča dating from 1310 are in a very similar style.

There is nothing to touch this realism, this worldliness, in the paintings of the Protaton on Mount Athos. None of the scenes there are rendered with greater solidity than that of the *Washing of the Feet* (Plate 77), none of the saintly or divine figures with greater realism than that of Jesus explaining to the Apostles the meaning of his action; no individual figure is more dramatic and expressive than the centurion in the *Crucifixion*. Yet on none of these occasions does the search for realism approach the degree that was achieved at Staro Nagoričino or in the Perebleptos at Ochrid. Nowhere on Athos does the three-dimensional conception, the dramatic nature or the everyday character of the figures equal that of the work of Michael and Eutychios in these churches in Macedonia. Indeed, there seems little possibility that the painter of the Protaton, call him Panseleinos or not as you will, is to be regarded as the same man who worked at Ochrid or Staro Nagoričino.

Could these men — Astrapas, Michael, Eutychios — have been Greeks from Salonica? It is hard to accept this. To the writer there seems to be an element in this Macedonian work which is distinct, and which can best be explained by associating it with the Slav upbringing of the artists concerned. Millet's Cretan school is essentially Greek; that which he termed the Macedonian is surely to be regarded as of a dual character. One branch, that which we see in Salonica, on Mount Athos, and in other places in Greece, though dramatic in contrast to the Cretan, remained fundamentally allied to Constantinople. The approach was still essentially spiritual at basis, and extremes of emotion and drama were avoided. In work of the other, that which we see in most of King Milutin's foundations, a more exaggerated, a more dramatic approach was favoured, and the paintings were more forceful, more material in outlook. It may be suggested that the differences we see here are to be attributed to the Slav patronage and training of the artists, even if they were Greeks by birth.

The decoration recently uncovered from beneath plaster of Turkish date in the church of the Virgin Ljeviska at Prizren is of a rather different character. The church is dated to between 1307 and 1309, some ten years later than the Perebleptos (St Clement) at Ochrid, and the paintings have usually been associated with those in Milutin's other churches because the name of Astrapas appears in the porch, in connection with a number of scenes done on a rather small scale. But the work here, even more so than that in the church itself, is very individual, and has already given rise to disputes with regard to date, for it seemed hard to equate these paintings, done between 1307 and 1309, with those at Ochrid done presumably in 1295, those in St Nikitas of 1307 and those at Staro Nagoričino of 1317. Surely the explanation is to be found in the fact that the majority of the work at Prizren is to be attributed to an entirely different hand? When we find Michael's work at Ochrid designated in an inscription as 'by the hand of Michael of Astrapas', it means that Michael was Astrapas' pupil; and it may further be interpreted as implying that Astrapas himself had nothing to do with the Ochrid paintings.

The paintings in the porch at Prizren are on a small scale, but are very lively and expressive and the individual figures, when isolated, are often of great quality, power and beauty. The work in the church itself is more monumental and on a very much grander scale, and stands out as the finest of the age in Yugoslavia, in spite

111

of the hackings which the plaster suffered when the church was converted into a mosque during the Turkish occupation. The work of three separate hands has been distinguished, one who is called the 'Master of the Passion', who did scenes in the naos, another who has been termed the 'George Master', who worked in the exonarthex, and finally the 'Master of the Prophets', who has been tentatively identified with Astrapas. He was a painter of great ability, but it is perhaps the *Passion Cycle*, whoever was responsible for it, that shows the finest work and the most able powers of composition; the scene of the *Communion of the Apostles* is by the same hand — it is both sympathetic and majestic, and at the same time fits ideally into the rather awkward space left for it by the curve of the arch (Plate 86).

The work of all three hands at Prizren, including, very probably, the portrait of King Milutin (Plate 88), stands rather apart from the style set by Michael and Eutychios at Ochrid, St Nikitas and Staro Nagoričino. It was this manner that was to the fore also at Studenica in 1314, in the large and impressive monastery church at Gračanica, around 1321, and finally at Dečani around 1327, where there is a decoration which surpasses all others in elaboration and in the mass of scenes that are illustrated; there are thus forty-six scenes from Genesis, forty-three from the Passion, a whole calendar in 365 scenes, and many others.

King Milutin's church at Studenica is a large building, its walls adorned with a considerable number of biblical scenes in several tiers, with full length figures of the saints below. The rendering of the *Birth of the Virgin* may be noted. It is a large composition, containing a mass of figures before an elaborate and solid architectural background. It tells the story clearly and is typical of the illustrative character of the work of this school. The *Anastasis* is akin, and is very expressive (Plate 87). Architecturally Gračanica is by far the most interesting of King Milutin's foundations; it dates from 1321, but the interior is somewhat oppressive. Its paintings are much gentler and calmer than those which bear the signatures of Michael and Eutychios and they seem to belong to a more truly Byzantine manner, as is indicated by the *St John Baptist* in the prothesis (Plate XIV). The rendering of the *Prophet Elias* is again conservative (Plate 90); so much so that it is tempting to suggest that the painter was a Greek. Queen Simonis, who was a Byzantine princess by birth, takes a prominent position among persons depicted, and it is possible that she even brought the artist with her to Serbia. In any case, realistic details are absent as, for instance, in the scene of the *Raising of Lazarus*, where the assistant who opens the coffin does not raise his cloak to his nose to allay the smell, a realistic feature typical of truly Macedonian iconography. The landscape backgrounds in many of the scenes suggest the influence of Constantinople in their fantasy, while the portrait of St John the Baptist noted above is close to that at Kariye or even to that in the earlier *Deesis* in Hagia Sophia at Constantinople. Details of the Judgement scene are vivid and decorative and suggest some ultimately more or less classical prototype conveyed perhaps via the medium of a bestiary.

At Gračanica the inscriptions are in Greek; in the church of St Demetrius at Peć, painted between 1317 and 1324, they are in Slav, and the painter was named John. Was he a Slav? One of the most delightful products of the painting of this age is imbued with a realism that would suggest that he was; it is the striking figure of a woman with a jug in the scene of the *Nativity of the Virgin* (Plate 89). It would seem however that the language of the inscriptions is not to be regarded as a very reliable guide to the nationality of the painters. Only when there are actual signatures in Slav can script be regarded as anything like a sure guide. Whether or not the converse is true, namely that signatures written in Greek imply that the painters were Greeks, is contested by Petković and upheld by Xyngopoulos. Logically Xyngopoulos should be correct, for Greek was for long the ecclesiastical language, but the conclusions we have reached above with regard to the work of Michael and Eutychios seem to refute this suggestion.

The church at Dečani was built at the behest of Stephen Uroš III, Dečanski, and was completed by his son Stephen Dušan, between 1329 and 1335. Its great size and considerable grandeur reflect the character of the age in which it was built, for it was at this time that Stephen finally secured the independence of his country and indeed succeeded in including much of the former Byzantine territory within the frontiers of his empire, as well as lands which had at times been claimed by the Bulgarians. The effect of the mass of paintings that decorate the interior of this church is somewhat overwhelming, but the work is gay and spirited in itself. The rendering of *Paradise* is particularly attractive, the colouring fresh and cheerful. Yet on the whole it is a narrative art, rather than an interpretational one — it tells the story clearly enough, but it does not move the spectator profoundly or inspire thoughts or emotions other than those associated with the actual theme.

If there is room for dispute regarding the nationality of some of the men responsible for the wall paintings of King Milutin's school, there would seem to be less possibility of argument in the case of the icons that were produced at the time, for there national characteristics are more clearly marked. Good examples are preserved in several of the monasteries, and there was an especially fine collection in the church of the Perebleptos (St Clement) at Ochrid; most of them are now in the Skopolje museum. Some of them are Byzantine, notably two double-sided icons which were presented by the Emperor Andronicos II Palaeologos around 1320 (see page 158)([10]). But others are local products, which are distinguished by a more dramatic approach, by a love of rhythmical compositions, by an angular treatment, by a rather more sombre colouring and by rather different proportions in the figures. The earliest example of the type is to be dated to the later years of the thirteenth century; it is a large double-sided icon, bearing the *Virgin and Child* on one face and the *Crucifixion* on the other (Plate 91). In respect of its deep, rich colouring and its monumental character it is akin to the wall paintings of Sopoćani, but the *Virgin* is more austere and the rendering of the *Crucifixion* more dramatic and emotional; Christ's body is quite severely contorted, John's pose is redolent of profound grief and the Virgin is bowed in sorrow([11]). In fact, we see here a work imbued with much of the grandeur of Sopoćani, blended with all the drama that characterises the Macedonian school, and to this is added the angularity and expression which are typical of so much Slav work in the Balkans. Among quite a number of icons done in this region around the year 1300, this is the first to show the characteristics of what may be fairly termed as the fully-fledged Yugoslav style of icon painting.

The Church of the Perebleptos at Ochrid boasted several other examples of the group. Most striking is a large icon of St Matthew (Plate 92) — it is as much as 106 centimetres high — and there are several smaller festival icons some of which are probably to be attributed to the same painter; they depict the *Nativity*, the *Baptism*, the *Ascent to Calvary*, the *Descent into Limbo*, the *Incredulity of Thomas*, *Pentecost*, the *Presentation of the Virgin in the Temple*, and the *Dormition of the Virgin* (Plates 94 and 95). In addition to the features noted, the backgrounds of all these icons are unusually pale in colour and the drawing is of a rather meticulous nature. All must have been produced in the same workshop, though different hands are to be distinguished. It has been suggested that some of them are to be assigned to either Michael or Eutychios, the wall-painters, but the respective hands of these men can hardly be identified for certain.

These panels represent the school of Ochrid, but other schools developed elsewhere, especially in the monasteries. One of the most interesting was at Zrze, where a painter called Makarios worked under the patronage of a local dignitary called Constantine Djurdjić; one of his best works was done late in his life, namely a remarkable rendering of the Virgin and Child, with the special designation, Pelagonitissa (Plate 96). The name is probably taken from that of a town now known as Bitolj or Monastir. Milković-Pepek has made a special study of it, and suggests that the pose was derived from that of the Virgin of Tenderness (*Umilenye*), though the strange, twisted attitude of the Child, with His back to the spectator, is to be regarded as a local peculiarity. The variant was especially popular in Yugoslavia, but it was not restricted to that country, for the same pose is assumed on a Greek icon in the monastery of St Catherine on Mount Sinai, and there is a variant where the pose is rather more restrained in the Monastery of Dochiariou on Mount Athos[12]. But the style of the Zrze painting, with its stress on angularity, is wholly Slav. Other icons which are to be assigned to Serbia or Macedonia are to be found in various collections throughout the country, and a famous panel bearing the Holy Face or Mandelion preserved in the Cathedral at Laon in France, has also been attributed to Yugoslavia. But on the whole the wall-paintings are more important than the panels; there are more of them, and they are mostly better preserved. The early fourteenth century saw Serbia's greatest glory, most rulers were zealous patrons of the arts, and the works that were executed were all of quality.

Around the middle of the fourteenth century, the wall-paintings often began to take on a more popular character, as we see for instance in those in the monasteries of Lesnovo, Marko and Matejić. The work can mostly be attributed to local painters. It is somewhat crude, but is always expressive and in many cases has considerable charm as well as being wholly sincere. The church at Lesnovo dates from 1341, but the narthex was added in 1349, and the paintings all belong to that date. They depict a full New Testament cycle as well as some scenes from the Old; the illustration to Psalm 150 is especially interesting for the text 'Praise him on the lute and harp' is illustrated in contemporary guise, with the crowd dancing a national dance, the 'Kolo', which is still danced in villages today (Plate 97). The same vigorous but popular style is to the fore in the decoration of Marko Manastir, which belongs to the later years of the fourteenth century. Several painters worked there, but all seem to have been able to add a personal touch to the old themes. The rendering of *Rachel's Lament* over her children is thus pathetic and profoundly expressive at the same time (Plate 98). The picture of St Blaise is more unusual, for it shows a distinct sense of humour — it is almost a caricature of some sly old monk of the day (Plate 95). The writings of the time speak of the difficult characters of some of the older monks and of the dance that they led the novices; this is clearly one of them, painted perhaps by a younger monk who had suffered under one of the older generation, but had at the same time the power to penetrate below his somewhat wry exterior.

Such paintings as survive in Greece itself are again to be classed under several heads, and both urban and local styles are to be found there. Though Xyngopoulos was no doubt correct when he assigned the paintings of the Protaton on Athos to a painter who had been taught in Salonica — whether or not his name was Panseleinos — it can hardly be claimed that the mass of paintings that survive in the smaller churches of northern Greece, notably those at Kastoria and Verroia, were also done by men from the great city; most of these paintings clearly bear the stamp of local workmanship. This is very obvious if an outstandingly fine icon of the *Crucifixion* from Salonica – now in the Byzantine museum at Athens (Plate 104) – is compared with any of the fourteenth-century paintings at Kastoria. The icon could pass as a Constantinopolitan work, so accomplished, so sophisticated is the feeling, even if the immensely tall Virgin and the sorrowing Apostle are perhaps more redolent of emotion than would have been usual in the capital, while the colouring is rather more sombre than it is, for example, in the wall painting at Kariye Camii. But there are, on the other hand, no hints whatsoever of the rather garish hues of the wall paintings in the Perebleptos (St Clement) at Ochrid.

Salonica would seem to have been an important centre of icon painting during this period, and there are several panels that can be associated with the city or its region on the evidence of inscriptions, though there is often little with regard to style that would serve to differentiate them. Most important is a panel bearing the figure of Christ now in the Hermitage at Leningrad (Plate 103). On the margins at either side are portraits of donors and an inscription which attests that the icon was painted for two brothers named Alexios and John, who lived in the region of the Nestos and Struma rivers, and were at one time associated with the monastery of the Pantocrator on Mount Athos; the icon was offered to the monastery by them, and must have been painted between 1360 and 1370. Its rather severe style associates it with Salonica rather than with Constantinople. Two other icons of Christ which were shown at the Byzantine exhibition at Athens in 1964 have been compared to this panel (Cat. nos. 200 and 201); the second, like the icon now in Leningrad, came from the monastery of the Pantocrator on Mount Athos; it and the other, which belongs to the church St Therapon at Mytilene, are perhaps rather later in date than that at Leningrad. An icon of the *Virgin and Child* from the church of the Prophet Elias at Verroia, which was also shown at the Byzantine exhibition in Athens in 1964 (no. 221), is again to be regarded as a Salonican product (Plate 101), as is a fine panel from Poganovo in Bulgaria which is now at Sofia([13]).

Wall paintings of the first half of the fourteenth century are comparatively numerous in northern Greece. Most of the work is in small churches and essentially provincial, but here and there decorations stand out, for example in some of the churches at Kastoria and Verroia, in both of which places they are surprisingly numerous; though they are all extremely small, they are all lavishly decorated([14]). There are also fragmentary paintings in most of the later churches at Salonica. Those which decorate the vertical walls of the Church of the Holy Apostles may be noted, for they are reasonably complete and of high quality, though not quite up to the standard of the mosaics in the dome and on the pendentives and vaults. They were done for the Patriarch Niphon between 1312 and 1315, under the direction of Abbot Paul. They are, like the mosaics in the dome and the pendentives, in a style closer to that prevailing at Constantinople at the time than to the work of King Milutin's school.

Last, but so far as quality is concerned by no means least, of the paintings at Salonica are those recently uncovered in a small, almost insignificant church close to the walls on the eastern fringe of the town; it bears the name of St Nicholas Orphanos. The paintings depict the *Twelve Feasts*, scenes from the Old and New Testaments, a *Passion* cycle, the *Akathystos Hymn*, scenes from the life of St Nicholas (Plate 99), and the figures of other saints (Plates XV and XVI). They are thus in accord with a very elaborate conception of church decoration, more in keeping with one of the great monastic churches of Athos than with the tiny building which they adorn. Xyngopoulos notes certain similarities with the paintings of Staro Nagoričino and on this basis suggests a date between 1310 and 1320[15]. This seems probable enough, but these exquisite, miniature-like wall paintings are closer in style to the icon paintings discussed a few paragraphs above than they are to the rather coarser large-scale wall paintings and they contrast very markedly with the work of Michael and Eutychios and their followers. The personal style of the painters at St Nicholas is especially to be noted in the way in which the faces are depicted, and it is here that these paintings appear at their best; often they are of very great beauty. The interest in movement, the stress that is laid on emotion, and the great fullness of the scenes that we see here are all features characteristic of the Macedonian school as a whole; it is perhaps the love of detail and their miniature-like character that distinguishes the paintings of St Nicholas Orphanos as Salonican.

Paintings that are either wholly in the manner of the Macedonian school, or which are closely related, are to be found in other parts of Greece, but there was much intermingling of styles, and it is virtually impossible to attempt any system of classification that is reliable – at best one can say with Sotiriou[16], that different 'manners' existed in different places rather than different schools. Work which is broadly Macedonian is thus to be found in Euboea, on the mainland, and even in Crete itself, during the first quarter of the fourteenth century; thereafter it is all more 'Greek' than it is anything else. Only seldom is this later work of any great artistic quality. One may thus distinguish a 'later Greek school', but it is impossible to subdivide it on either a geographical or a truly stylistic basis, though here and there certain later works stand out, as for example those at Mistra, which are of the very highest quality, for Mistra boasted a civilisation perhaps even more advanced than that of the capital itself; the Mistra paintings will be discussed in the final chapter.

5

The Flowering of the Metropolitan School in the Fourteenth Century

The Greek writers speak with horror of the period of Latin supremacy at Constantinople, and what they have to say reflects more seriously on the lack of culture of the Latins than on their political shortcomings. The Blachernae Palace, where the rulers had their residence, was thus left not only in a state of disrepair at their departure, but also in one of dirt and filth; many of the churches that had been taken over were dilapidated, and there seems no reason to believe that the Latins played any very active role as patrons of art between 1204 and 1261. Though many of the Greek churches were converted to the Latin cult, no traces of Latin adornments survive other than the long series of tombstones from the building in Galata know as Arap Camii, which was built as and always remained a Latin church. Some fragments of painted and stained glass recently discovered in the Church of the Pantocrator (Zierek Camii), which at first glance look Latin, have been claimed as Byzantine by Megaw [1], and though this view has been questioned, a date in the twelfth century has been firmly established on reliable archaeological evidence. Nothing else on a large scale which can definitely be dated to these years survives. It seems possible, however, that a certain number of small-scale works may have been made in Constantinople for Orthodox patrons, and Weitzmann, as we have seen, has distinguished a group of miniatures, examples of which are to be assigned to the thirteenth century; the most important of them is a copy of the Gospels in the British Museum, dated to 1285 (Burney 20), the miniatures of which are fresh and brilliant but somewhat clumsy. One fact is nevertheless patently clear, namely that around the year 1300 there was a tremendous burst of artistic activity in Constantinople, and though a very great deal has perished or was destroyed when churches were turned into mosques, enough survives to attest to the universally high standard that pertained in the capital, while the mosaic and painted decoration of one monument is to be classed as one of the most outstanding works of art of all time. This is the little church we usually know by its Turkish name of Kariye Camii. The mosaics and painting were probably executed between about 1315 and 1320. No more impressive example of the closeness of the association between a building and its decoration is to be found in the Byzantine world, for the multiplicity of domes, vaults and arches provide an ideal setting for the scintillating colours of the mosaics.

The Church of the Saviour in Chora, to give Kariye Camii its Greek name, consists of a main sanctuary, square on plan and domed, which is preceded by two transverse narthices; the outer one also extends across the western end of a side aisle or parecclesion, virtually a separate church beside the main one on the southern side. The parecclesion is adorned with paintings, the main church and the two narthices with mosaics(²). At some time or another the dome of the main church fell, so that little of the original decoration survives in the central area. The dome was no doubt occupied by the usual bust of Christ Pantocrator, while the principal feasts of the church probably covered the vaults. Only one of these scenes now survives, the *Dormition of the Virgin* over the western door. The work is distinguished by its small proportions and delicacy, as well as by rather bulging foreheads and pin-point eyes of the figures (Plate 102). It is a lovely mosaic, but is surpassed in beauty by panels on either side of the apse, which show Christ to the north and the Virgin and Child to the south (Plate XVIII). Both have now been cleaned by the Byzantine Institute of America, and both – especially the panel with the Virgin and Child – are works of rare delight; it is absurd to suppose that an art so exquisite could ever have been born simply out of the void of the Latin conquest.

We have already called attention to the great panel bearing the *Deesis* or rather the two figures of Christ and the Virgin, with the portraits of Isaac Comnenos Porphyrogenitus and the nun Melane below, for we mentioned it in connection with the problem of dating the *Deesis* in Hagia Sophia (see p. 29). It is a large composition, larger in scale than anything else at Kariye and occupies the eastern wall of the southern bay of the inner narthex (Plate 100). At one time it was thought that it was earlier in date than the other mosaics in the church, partly on stylistic grounds and partly because fragments of an inscription were visible which referred to Isaac Comnenos. This was Isaac II who restored the church between 1185 and 1195 with the intention of being buried there, and it was thought that the mosaic must have been set up by him. But cleaning has shown not only that the work is stylistically wholly typical of the early fourteenth century, but also that the plaster of the setting bed of the part on which Isaac is depicted overlies that on the opposite side, where the nun Melane is shown, and therefore cannot be earlier in date. But the inscription associated with the nun informs us that she is in all probability to be identified as the Princess Maria Palaeologina, daughter of Michael VIII Palaeologos (1259–82); she was married to the Mongol Khan Abagu in 1265(³). On his death in 1281 she returned to Constantinople, where she founded the church of St Mary of the Mongols – the only Byzantine church in Constantinople which has remained in Christian usage throughout the whole period since 1453. She became a nun in 1307, so that the mosaic on which she is depicted in nun's costume must be later than that year. The *Deesis* panel thus forms beyond any doubt a part of the main decoration of the church, and must have been done after 1308.

There are a few other panels on a similar monumental scale, notably one of *Christ Blessing* over the door leading from the outer to the inner narthex accompanied by an inscription identifying him as ἡ χώρά τῶν ξώντων. On the lunette opposite is the Virgin with the inscription ἡ χώρά τῶν ἀγωρήτῶν, which may be translated respectively as 'the abode of the living' and 'the abode of the unsullied'. The church no doubt derived its name from the former appelation rather than from any association with a location 'in the fields', as was at one time proposed on the assumption that it was an early foundation which originally stood outside the walls – presumably the walls of Constantine, for the Theodosian walls must always have enclosed it. Christ is designated in the same way on another panel which occupies the lunette over the door from the inner narthex to the church, but here Theodore Metochites, who was responsible for commissioning the decoration and for the repairs to the church which began around 1305, is shown at one side offering its model to Christ (Plate 105). His remarkable head-dress was granted to him as a special distinction by Andronicos II; later he was thrown into disgrace and ended his days as a monk worshipping in the church which he had formerly endowed.

Close to the first of these figures of Christ are the *Miracles of the Turning of the Water into Wine* and of the *Loaves and Fishes*, symbolic of Christ's character as the Giver of Life (Plate 106). The date of 1303 in Arabic figures has been read on the former, but it is probably no date at all, but only a decorative pattern. Among the portraits of saints on the pilasters and in medallions at the lower levels there are many that are very lovely. The majority of the mosaics are however devoted to recording the story of Christ's and the Virgin's lives in great detail. The story begins in the first bay to the north of the inner narthex, where the life of the Virgin is depicted as recorded in the Apocryphal Protoevangelion of St James. In the dome she appears as Theotokos, the Bringer-forth of God, supported by sixteen ancestors of Christ and a number of prophets. Below in the south-eastern pendentive, Joachim, Mary's father, is depicted with his sheep, mourning that he is childless.

In the eastern lunette is the *Annunciation to St Anne* (Plate 108); and a later scene from the story, the *Judgement of Mary*. The story continues on the soffit of the arch separating this bay from the next with the scene of the *Meeting of Anna and Joachim* and other events from Joachim's life. In the second bay are shown the *Birth of Mary*, *Mary Taking her First Seven Steps*, *Mary Blessed by the Priests*, *Mary Caressed by her Parents*, and another subsequent scene, the *Choice of Joseph*. In the scene of the *First Steps* the childlike figure, in its long heavy robes, is both charming and beautiful (Plate 110). An interesting feature is the nurse's shawl blown over her head by the wind; it is a very old motif derived from some classical proto-type, and appears time and again in Byzantine art. In the third bay Mary is given wool to weave the Veil of the Temple; she is taken into the Temple (Plate 109) and there receives bread from the Archangel Gabriel.

The story of Christ's life begins in the first bay at the northern end of the outer narthex, with *Joseph's Dream* and the *Journey from Nazareth to Bethlehem* (Plate 107). The depiction of the journey is particularly lovely as a picture – glorious in colour and very effective in composition, but it is perhaps surpassed by the *Numbering of the People*, where Joseph and Mary are registered before Cyrenius (Plate 111). It is a particularly vivid and delightful composition, for the timidity of the Virgin, the anxiety of Joseph that she conduct herself to the best advantage, the rather bored preoccupation of the guard who beckons her into place with his sword, and the careful zeal of the clerk are all admirably rendered. Mary and Joseph then attend the Passover in Jerusalem.

In the second bay are a number of scenes that were rather more frequently depicted – the *Nativity*, the *Return of the Holy Family from Egypt to Nazareth*, the *Baptism*, and the scenes of *Our Lord's Temptation*. The *Nativity* is rendered with real understanding of the event (Plate 112); the figure of the Virgin is espec-ially sympathetic, for she is conceived as a gentle, suffering woman rather than a monumental goddess, as was usual in the tenth and eleventh centuries; the scene at Daphni may for instance be compared (Plate 2). The story continues in the fourth bay, for the central one is devoted to the portraits of Christ and the donor as already described. Here the magi ride towards Jerusalem, guided by the star, and appear before Herod, while Elizabeth, fleeing with her child John, follows. The previous scene, the *Annunciation to Elizabeth at the Well*, is especially effective, as is the *Annunciation to St Anne* (Plate 108). In the fifth bay Herod enquires about Christ's birth from the priests, and women mourn the death of their children. Of the miracles one of the most impressive is that of the *Marriage at Cana*, which is particularly full and vivid (Plate XX).

The outer narthex extends not only across the whole width of the main church, but also across the western end of the parecclesion; it thus has one more bay than the inner narthex. In the central dome Christ appears as Pantocrator with the prophets below on the walls; the scenes include the *Massacre of the Innocents* and a number of Christ's miracles. They bring to an end the story of Christ's Life; the absence of the major feasts — the *Transfiguration*, the *Entry into Jerusalem* and so on, as well as that of subjects from the Passion cycle — supports the suggestion made above, that these subjects were probably treated in the body of the church itself.

The jewel-like richness of these mosaics and the glowing beauty of the colours has to be seen to be realised, but though these factors to some extent account for the overwhelming effect of these mosaics, the mastery of design and quality of the draughtsmanship are also outstanding and serve to make this decoration one of the greatest glories of art for which the fourteenth century was responsible. And these features are also to the fore in the decoration of the parecclesion, even if the jewel-like effect of the mosaics is lacking, for there the work is in paint. It was executed at much the same date as that in the church and the masters must have been trained in the same school; it has even been suggested that the same men were responsible, though this hardly seems likely. Here many of the scenes depicted are very unusual ones, for which few, if any, parallels exist elsewhere. Most of them are concerned with the after-life, in accordance with the character of the chapel which was intended for funerary purposes — there are a series of grave-niches or arcasolia along its walls.

Most appropriately the *Resurrection*, rendered according to Byzantine tradition by the *Descent of Christ to Limbo*, occupies the conch of the apse (Plate XIX). The painting is one of the most beautiful that have survived in the whole of Byzantine art. It is redolent of hope and comfort, a thing of very great loveliness and profound significance, for Christ's action in raising Adam and Eve symbolises the hope of Resurrection for all. Other scenes connected with the same theme were shown on the arch of the sanctuary. Thus *Christ Raises Jairus's Daughter* to the right and the *Widow's Son* to the left; both are in poor condition.

On the large vault to the west of this was shown the *Last Judgement* and the *Second Coming of Christ* (Plate 113), with numerous scenes of death, torment and judgement around, including a strange rendering of the worm that corrupteth and the flame that devoureth, almost tachiste in appearance. Especially striking is the rendering of the scroll of heaven, a visionary conception suggestive of the mind and brush of el Greco (Plate 114). In the small pendentives below are scenes connected with the Judgement — the *Rich Man in Hell*, the *Land and Sea Surrendering their Dead*, the *Angel Conducting Lazarus to Abraham*, and *Abraham and the Souls in Paradise*. In the main pendentives of the dome are four hymnographers, *St John Damascenos*, *St Cosmas*, *St Joseph* and *St Theophanes*. At a first glance they have very much the appearance of the Evangelists; and the Evangelist compositions so popular as a decoration for the pendentives in mid and later Byzantine art may well have served as models. In the lunettes are other scenes — that of the *Ark of the Covenant*, borne aloft by four bearers, may be noted, for it forms a fine and impressive composition, full of life and movement.

The decoration of the dome which roofs the more westerly compartment of the parecclesion follows a more usual theme — the Virgin and Child at the centre in the pose known as the Nikopea, supported by twelve angels; these and the windows

Ο ΗΙΕ̣ΜΟΣ

82 Staro Nagoričino, Macedonia. Wall painting;
the *Mocking of Christ*; 1317–8.

83 *(left)* Ochrid, Macedonia. Church of the Perebleptos (St Clement). Wall painting; the *Betrayal*; c. 1295.

84 *(below left)* Ochrid, Macedonia. Church of the Perebleptos (St Clement). Wall painting; the *Dormition of the Virgin*; c. 1295.

85 *(opposite above)* Čučer, Macedonia. Church of St Nikitas. Wall painting; the *Cleansing of the Temple*; 1307.

86 *(opposite below)* Prizren, Macedonia. Church of the Mother of God, Ljeviska. Wall painting; the *Communion of the Apostles*; c. 1309.

ХЬ ИЗГОНТЬ ПРОДАЮЩЕЕ ИКОУПОУ
ЮЩЕ(Е)НЗЦ(Р)КВЕ

IC XC

87 (left) Studenica, Serbia. King Milutin's Church. Wall painting; the *Anastasis*; 1313–4.

88 (below left) Prizren, Macedonia. Church of the Mother of God, Ljeviska. Wall painting; portrait of the founder, *King Milutin*; c. 1309.

89 (below right) Peć, Serbia. Church of St Demetrius. Detail from the scene of the *Birth of the Virgin*. 1317–24.

90 Gračanica, Serbia. Wall painting; the *Prophet Elias*; 1321.

91 Icon. The *Crucifixion*; early fourteenth century. Formerly in the
Church of the Perebleptos (St Clement), Ochrid.

92 *(above left)* Icon. *St Mathew;* early fourteenth century. Macedonian State
Collections; formerly in the Church of the Perebleptos (St Clement), Ochrid.

93 *(above right)* The Monastery of Marko, Serbia. *St. Blaise.* 1386–95.

94, 95 Icons. Macedonian State Collection; formerly in the church of the Perebleptos (St Clement), Ochrid;
early fourteenth century. *(below left)* the *Anastasis.(below right) Doubting Thomas.*

96 Icon. The *Virgin Pelagonitissa*; Zrze, Macedonia;
early fourteenth century.

97 The Monastery Church, Lesnovo, Serbia.
Wall painting; *Psalm 150* 1341–9.

133

98 The Monastery of Marko, Serbia. Wall painting; *Rachel's Lament* 1386–95.

99 *(below)* Salonica, Curch of St Nicholas Orphanos. Wall painting; a scene from the *Life of St Nicholas*; early fourteenth century.

100 *(above)* Constantinople, Kariye Camii. Mosaic; the *Deesis Panel*; c. 1315.

101 *(above right)* Icon. The *Virgin Hodegetria*; early fourteenth century. From the Church of the Prophet Elias, Verroia, Greece.

102 *(right)* Constantinople, Kariye Camii. Mosaic; the *Dormition of the Virgin*. (Before cleaning) c. 1315.

ΙϹ Ο ΠΑΝΤΟ ΧϹ ΚΡΑΤω

103 Icon. *Christ Pantocrator* c. 1360–70. The Hermitage Museum, Leningrad.

104 Icon. The *Crucifixion*; early fourteenth century. The Byzantine Museum, Athens.

105, 106 Constantinople, Kariye Camii. Mosaics; c. 1315 (left) Christ and the donor, Theodore Metochites; (below left) the Miracle of the Loaves and Fishes.

107,108, 109 Constantinople, Kariye Camii. Mosaics; c. 1315. (*right*) the *Journey to Bethlehem*; (*centre right*) the *Annunciation to St Anne*; (*bottom right*) the *Introduction of Mary into the Temple*.

HΠTABHMATIΣYCA

110, 111, 112 Constantinople, Kariye, Camii. Mosaics; c. 1315. *(above) Mary's first steps*; *(opposite above)* the *Numbering of the People*; *(opposite below)* the *Nativity*.

113, 114 Constantinople, Kariye Camii. Parecclesion.
(*above*) Painting in the vault; the *Last Judgement*; c. 1320.
(*opposite*) Detail of the painting in the vault; the *Seal of Heaven*; c. 1320.

115 Constantinople, Kariye Camii. Parecclesion.
Painting in the dome; c. 1320.

116 Constantinople, Kilisse Camii. Mosaics in the narthex; *Kings of Israel*;
early fourteenth century.

117 *(top left)* Constantinople, Fetiye Camii. Mosaic in the dome; *The Pantocrator*; c. 1315.

118 *(above left)* Salonica, Church of the Holy Apostles. Mosaic; the *Transfiguration*; c. 1312.

119, 120 Miniature mosaics; *(top right) Christ of Pity*, early fourteenth century. The Monastery of Tatarna, Greece; *(bottom right) the Annunciation*; c. 1320. The Victoria and Albert Museum, London.

146

121 Murano, near Venice.
Church of St Donato.
Mosaic in the apse; the
Virgin; early fourteenth
century.

122 Panel painting: from the Visotsky Chin; *St Peter*; 1387–95. The Tretyakov Gallery, Moscow.

123 *(right)* Icon. *Christ in Majesty*; ascribed to Andrew Rublev and Daniel Cheorny; c. 1408.

below them are separated by ribs adorned with decorative patterns of great beauty and variety, all of which seem to have been done freehand, without the aid of stencils (Plate 115). The nature of the designs is surprising, for one would at first glance have tended to assign them to Italy and to a much later date than one around 1310. Grabar indeed suggests that the whole decoration of the dome, both the designs and the actual division into compartments by ribs is, at Kariye, the result of Italian influence, and he cites thirteenth-century parallels at Nepi, Anagni and elsewhere in support of his thesis(⁴). The ribs, however, are also found in Moslem work. That there are similarities to Italy cannot be disputed, but if the thesis of eastern priorities in style proposed in the preceding chapters is accepted, the links in this case might also be expected to run from east to west rather than in the opposite direction; or it may well be that there were parallel developments from earlier prototypes in both regions. It must never be forgotten that our knowledge is very incomplete and that much more has been destroyed in the East than in the West.

On the lower parts of the walls are paintings which are in no way inferior in quality to those above, though they are perhaps less inspiring. In the body of the church are full-length figures of saints, most of them military; the *Head of St Sabas Stratelates* is perhaps the finest of them, but all are imbued with dignity of a rather classical character. In the apse are the *Fathers of the Church* and on a panel at the same level to the north, a lovely figure of the *Virgin*. Quite a considerable portion of the wall space is taken up also by the tomb niches or arcasolia; there are two on each side of the parecclesion and others along the western wall of the outer narthex, under the windows. They contained, on the back walls and on the side arches, portraits of the deceased. Most of these portraits are in a very battered condition, but the figures are interesting, if only because of the patterned silks they wear. In one case the robes depict a stuff adorned with eagles and the initials of the Palaeologan family, Π A, treated as a monogram.

It is interesting to note that these mosaics and paintings were being done almost at the same time that Giotto was painting his well-known frescoes in the Arena Chapel at Padua. In many cases his rendering of the scenes was, iconographically speaking, wellnigh identical with those at Kariye or in some other Byzantine work of the period, and certain of Giotto's technical mannerisms were also closely akin. But the lines of development taken in the east and west around 1300 were distinct; the east remained true to an etherial, transcendental, other-worldly approach, concentrating primarily on the spiritual, while Giotto sought for realism, solidity and actuality with an energy which was wholly western, and he introduced a number of new ideas to further his aims. Thus at Kariye the artists still retained the old system of perspective, where the picture was conceived from within rather than from outside(⁵); Giotto, on the other hand, was already experimenting with vanishing perspective of a western type. The Kariye painters were undoubtedly deeply concerned with humanism, for their art is not aloof and hieratic as was at one time supposed, but they nevertheless still lived to some extent in an unreal world; Giotto was at the same time humanist and realist. But the most profound difference which was thereafter to separate the art of the west from that of the Byzantine world was one of conception, for in the west the religious picture was intended to inform, record or inspire, or even to express the artist's interpretation of the theme, whereas in the east it played the part of a spiritual intermediary between the human and the divine, between this world and the next, and the artist's personality was not allowed to play any part. What may be termed the spiritual responsibility of art was never felt in the west to the same degree as in the Orthodox world, and therefore, with Giotto's experiments in the way of realism accomplished, art was free to develop along a course of realistic representation which was quite foreign to any possible line of progress in the east. There art could never wholly forsake its spiritual aims. It might seek a closer coordination between man and his natural surroundings, as it did at Kariye; new ideas of scale could be developed, where the figures, irrespective of their hierarchical importance, and the buildings, irrespective of their nature, could be brought into a more or less natural relationship one with the other — but always in the east the spiritual essence, the role of intermediary between this world and the next was there as the basic element. We can see this in the charming scene of the introduction of the Virgin into the Temple at Kariye, for the spiritual character of the scene is attested not only by the nature of the figures but also by the colouring, where light emanates from the figures themselves rather than from any wholly natural source. At times indeed it would seem that the idea of a mystic, uncreated light, which was at the basis of the religious teachings of a group known as the Hesychasts, was reflected in the art of the age, and the effects of their approach are to be seen not only on Mount Athos, where Hesychasm had its most ardent followers, but in the larger cities also, and not least in Constantinople[6].

Whether it was due to Hesychast beliefs or not, the essentially spiritual basis of art in the east served to differentiate it from that in the west in another respect, namely the greater importance that was accorded in the west to the individual. Though in Macedonia the names of artists began to be recorded around 1200, and we know the names of quite a number of painters of the thirteenth century, in Constantinople they were still suppressed and we know nothing of the names, still less anything of the personalities, of the men who produced the mosaics of Kariye or other works of the same date. Yet the eastern paintings and mosaics do not wholly lack the imprint of individual handling, and the next series of mosaics that can be studied in the capital, those in the Church of the Virgin Pammakaristos, better known as Fetiye Camii, are quite distinct in style from those at Kariye, though they too are wholly metropolitan and were done at almost exactly the same date.

The church was endowed by one Michael Glabas at the end of the thirteenth century, and early in the fourteenth a small chapel was added at the south-east corner of the church to serve as his mausoleum; he died in 1315 and the mosaics must belong to that year or to the next. The building is more or less square in plan, with a central dome, and three apses. The dome was originally supported on four columns, though the two to the north were removed and replaced by a large arch spanning the north side from wall to wall when the church became a mosque in the sixteenth century. In the dome is a mosaic of the Pantocrator, with twelve prophets below (Plate 117); it has been known for many years, for it never seems to have been covered over, in contrast with the mosaics on the walls and in a series of niches below. Here a number of saints were depicted, as well as eight scenes from Christ's life. In the apse Christ was shown for a second time, though figures of the Virgin on the wall to the north and of St John the Baptist on the wall to the south made this into a composition of the *Deesis* and not a second rendering of Christ as Pantocrator; he is indeed here described as Hyperagathos[7]. The choice of this scene rather than the Virgin and Archangels is probably due to the fact that the mosaic adorned a funerary chapel; the Virgin and St John would intercede with Christ for the soul of the deceased. The mosaics and marble revetments of the lower walls have all perished, but portions of the mosaics at the upper levels survive. The figures depict prophets and bishops and are comparatively well preserved; of the scenes only the *Baptism* survives[7]. All the mosaics have now been well cleaned and consolidated by the Byzantine Institute of America. They are very bright in colour, but the treatment is rather harder, the drawing less fluid than at Kariye, and it would seem that a distinct workshop, not only a different master, must have been involved. The work is also on a smaller, more intimate scale, for the space at the disposal of the mosaicist was very restricted. On the whole the work lacks the flowing delicacy both of Kariye and also of the best of the miniature mosaics of the period, like that of the *Annunciation* in the Victoria and Albert Museum (Plate 120).

Vestiges of yet another decoration of much the same date, but rather coarser workmanship, survive in the domes of the outer narthex of another church, Kilisse Camii, a building usually identified as the church of St Theodore Tyro. The work of cleaning is not yet complete. Enough is however visible to indicate that different men again must have worked here; the cubes are larger, the technique rather coarser, the drawing less accomplished (Plate 116). Indeed, all three decorations are distinct, and a comparison of them suggests that there must have been a good deal of stylistic variation between the workshops operating in the capital at the time, even though the general character of the art is the same.

Records or meagre traces show that other churches in Constantinople were also adorned early in the fourteenth century, and it may be that further decorations will be brought to light in the course of time. Till that day comes we may call attention to the closely related mosaics in the dome of the Church of the Holy Apostles at Salonica, which date from between 1312 and 1315[8]. The walls below are covered with frescoes (see p. 115). The elongated figures, the large heads with bulging foreheads, the small, deep-set eyes and bodies full at the middle and slender below are common both to Salonica and to Constantinople. The architectural backgrounds at Salonica are, however, rather less fantastic and imaginative than those at Kariye and there is perhaps a somewhat greater stress on expression and a more marked realism. In the *Entry into Jerusalem*, for example, the crowd is rather more dynamic than are the crowds at Kariye; the buildings are more solid, while the movement tends to be more vigorous. But in such scenes as the *Transfiguration* (Plate 118) it is hard to see differences which are much more marked than say those between Kariye and Fetiye, or to see in the mosaics of the Holy Apostles anything that would warrant their attribution to a distinct school in Salonica.

That work went on throughout the century is attested not only by the continuance of the Constantinopolitan style at Mistra, where the last and perhaps the finest decoration is dated to 1428, but also by records which state that no less than 40 churches in Constantinople, Galata and Chalcedon contained paintings which were done by an artist named Theophanes before he went to Russia. This was the famous Theophanes the Greek, who worked in the Church of the Transfiguration at Novgorod in 1378 (see pp. 165 f.). Unfortunately nothing that can be attributed to him survives in the Byzantine capital, though it has been suggested that his style must have been close to that of the painter of the parecclesion at Kariye. In Russia he developed a very personal manner, splashing on highlights with astonishing bravura much in the way that another Greek, Domenikos Theotokopoulos, better known perhaps as el Greco, was to do at a later date in Spain. There is, however, some work in Bulgaria which is related both to that done by Theophanes in Russia and even more closely to that which survives in the Byzantine capital.

This work is to be found in the principal rock-cut chapel near Ivanovo on the river Lom[9], and serves to indicate how widely spread was the influence of the metropolitan style even at this late date, when the Byzantine capital itself was impoverished and the empire had virtually ceased to exist. Though dated to around 1340, these paintings still retain something of the monumental character of those at Sopoćani, while the interest in muscles that is to be seen in the renderings of nude figures may be compared to that which characterised some of the work in Hagia Sophia at Trebizond, notably in the figures of the apostles in the scenes of the *Incredulity of Thomas* and the *Appearance of Christ on the Shores of Lake Tiberias* (Plate 60). Taken as a whole however the Ivanovo paintings are virtually direct descendants of those at Kariye.

Another interesting work in the same style on the periphery of the Byzantine world is the mosaic of the Virgin in the apse of the Church of San Donato on the island of Murano near Venice (Plate 121). Here the Virgin is shown alone without the child, but the figure is very elongated and the face is gentle and tender. The mosaic was at one time assigned to the twelfth century, but it can hardly be so early, for the style is close to Kariye. There are of course also a good many mosaics in St Mark's, which must be dated later than the original decoration there, for work went on more or less continuously till the sixteenth century, but after the twelfth it was all in a semi-western style, quite different from that of the Murano mosaic, and there is little evidence to suggest that the Venetian mosaic workers had adopted the delicate, picturesque manner characteristic of Kariye. It would therefore seem likely that the Murano mosaic was done either by a Greek immigrant or by a man who had studied in Constantinople under a Greek master.

Though the sumptuous works in gold and silver, enamel and precious stones, which were so characteristic of Byzantine art in the great Macedonian period, were in general beyond the resources of the Palaeologue age, some lovely books were illuminated, like that in the name of John Cantacuzenos, now in the Bibliothèque Nationale (Gr. 1242) (Plate 167); and one art of a very precious character was practised, namely that of the making of miniature mosaics, where tiny cubes of glass or semi-precious stone, often no bigger than a pin's head, were set in wax on a wooden board. The work is astonishingly minute and painstaking, though not intrinsically as expensive as enamelling on gold. Examples that are to be assigned to the fourteenth century are comparatively numerous and are to be found in quite a number of collections; one bearing the *Annunciation* in the Victoria and Albert Museum is typical; in style it is close to the mosaics of Kariye and it is probably to be assigned to the same workshop and certainly to Constantinople and to much the same date (Plate 120). A panel with the Forty Martyrs and another with St John Chrysostom at Dumbarton Oaks (Plate XVII), one with St Theodore in the Vatican, several at Vatopedi on Mount Athos, and a number of others elsewhere are definitely of the fourteenth century[10]. Though it is sadly battered, one of the less well known examples may be illustrated, for it has only recently been published in connection with the Byzantine exhibition at Athens in 1964. It is in the monastery of Tatarna at Evrytania (Exn. no. 167, Plate 119). It depicts *Christ, the Man of Sorrows*, a theme which had begun to appear in Byzantine art in the thirteenth century, as, for example, at Gradac in Serbia[11], though it was never as popular in the Orthodox world as in the West.

A few of these miniature mosaics are certainly to be dated earlier than the fourteenth century, like the panels bearing St Nicholas at Aachen (Byz. Ex. No. 161) and in the monastery on Patmos (Byz. Ex. No. 162); others give rise to discussion. An unusually large one in the Louvre (Byz. Ex. No. 163) showing the *Transfiguration* is wholly monumental as regards its composition and on that basis

might be assigned to the eleventh century, though the actual figures are more vivid and savour of the fourteenth; this mixed style and the dramatic nature of the detail suggest Salonica as a possible provenance, and a date around 1300 seems likely. A dating problem of rather different character arises with regard to a small panel of the *Virgin and Child* now in Santa Maria della Salute at Venice; here the style is wholly that of the Revival, but an inscription on the back gives the date as 1115 and states that the mosaic was given to the Emperor Manuel and was preserved in Hagia Sophia at Constantinople. But the inscription only belongs to the seventeenth century and is hardly to be relied upon as evidence of date. The mosaic was no doubt made in Constantinople.

The painted panels of this age that are to be assigned to Constantinople are fairly numerous. Quite a number are preserved in Russia, where many were taken at the time of their execution; others have recently been discovered among the rich collection in the Monastery of St Catherine on Mount Sinai; a few have at one time or another found their way into western museums and treasuries. Most important among those preserved in Russia are seven icons depicting Christ, the Virgin, St John, two archangels and two apostles that form a part of what is called the 'Visotsky Chin' (an upper row of the full size iconostasis) from the Chudov monastery in Russia (Plate 122). The panels were commissioned in Constantinople by Athanasius Visotsky. He arrived in the Byzantine capital in 1387 and took the panels back to Novgorod before 1395, so that their date is firmly fixed between these years. Three more icons are also mentioned, but these no longer survive. The colours are rather dark, the figures somewhat severe and quite distinct from those that characterise Russian work of the time. Though there is some variation in the style of the seven icons that survive, Lazarev, who was the first to publish them, believes that all are to be attributed to the same master[12]. He notes their similarity to wall paintings in Georgia done between 1384 and 1396, for which a Byzantine painter was also responsible, as well as a more general relationship to the work of Theophanes the Greek.

Other Byzantine icons now in Russia, but regarding which there is no documentation, include a small but lovely one of the *Dormition of the Virgin* (Plate XXIV), and another depicting the *Assembly of the Apostles*, both in the Museum of Fine Art at Moscow. The latter is of great beauty and the formal, rather severe, arrangement of the figures shows how a composition which might seem monotonous and dull can be rendered with delicacy and expression by the hand of a master, so that it is at the same time meaningful and lovely[13].

Outside Russia a particularly delightful little panel of the *Archangel Michael* in the Gallery at Pisa (Plate 124) may be noted. The archangel holds the scales of judgement in his hand, while a vigorous little black devil tries to weigh down one side to capture the soul of its occupant for torment. Black devils of this type were quite frequently depicted in Byzantine painting; one that is wellnigh identical appears among the paintings of Hagia Sophia at Trebizond, coming out of the mouth of the Woman of Canaan's daughter (Plate V). The icon is certainly a Constantinopolitan work, but there is no record as to when or how it got to Pisa.

Even more beautiful, the finest perhaps of all the icons exported from Constantinople at this time, is one that was till recently preserved in the Church of St Clement at Ochrid in Yugoslavia; it is now in the Skopolje Museum. It must have been a processional icon, for it is painted on both sides, on one face the Virgin designated as the *Saviour of Souls*, on the other the *Annunciation*. It is a painting of quite exceptional loveliness, wholly metropolitan in character (Plate XXV). It was prob-

XXIV Icon. The *Dormition of the Virgin*; early fourteenth century. The Museum of Fine Arts, Moscow.

ably done for the Monastery of Our Lady Psychosostria, Saviour of Souls, at Constantinople, and presented to Archbishop Gregory of Ochrid by John Cantacuzenos for a monastery of the same name which the Archbishop founded shortly before 1350([14]). Slightly later in date, though more austere, is an icon of the Archangel Michael, now in the Byzantine Museum at Athens (Byz. Ex. No. 225) (Plate 125). He holds a crystal orb, admirably painted, on which is a cross and the letters ΧΔΚ, which probably stand for the words Χρίςτος Δίκαιος Κριτης. This again is surely a Constantinopolitan work, and like most other products of the capital is not only of great technical excellence, but is imbued with a spirit of grandeur and serenity not usually to be encountered elsewhere — paintings done at Salonica are more dramatic, Russian ones more colourful and sweeter.

The exportation of panels from the capital seems to have continued at least till the Turkish conquest of 1453. Cardinal Bessarion's famous reliquary in the Academia at Venice (Byz. Ex. No. 187) or rather, the painted portion of it, was taken to Italy by him and presented to the Scuola della Carita in Venice around 1470, though it was painted in the previous century. It too is to be counted a Constantinopolitan work, as is a lovely icon of the *Adoration* in the Uffizi which must date from the earlier fifteenth century. There are several icons in the large collection in the museum attached to the church of San Giorgio dei Greci at Venice of similar date; the most interesting is one of the Pantocrator which was brought from Constantinople by the Grand Duchess Anne Notaras, who went to Venice as a refugee after the Turkish Conquest of 1453 and died there in 1507([15]). But of all these later icons there is none that surpasses in quality a panel of the Virgin now in the Tretyakov Gallery at Moscow, known as *Our Lady of Prinen* (Plate 126). It is to be dated to the end of the fourteenth or the beginning of the fifteenth century, and in its gentle reticence and wholly spiritual quality it remains unsurpassed. It represents for us the last truly great work that we know to have been produced in the capital.

6

The Beginnings of Painting in Russia

The earliest examples of Christian art that exist in Russia are the mosaics and wall-paintings of Hagia Sophia at Kiev, the former dating from between 1042 and 1046, the latter from around 1064; they are just as much Byzantine works on foreign soil as are the mosaics of Cefalù and Palermo in Sicily. In the twelfth century, as we have seen, Russian patrons were still ordering works of art in the Byzantine capital; both the icon *Our Lady of Vladimir*, an actual import, and the frescoes in the Cathedral at Vladimir, which are obvious products of the twelfth century Byzantine Revival, attest this. But there are other works of the twelfth or indeed even of the eleventh century which, though basically Byzantine, at the same time comprise elements which are to be regarded as truly Russian; they represent the contribution of local artists who must have been trained by immigrant Greeks, but who also gave to art something that was both original and indigenous; it is in work of this type that the first developments toward the formation of a distinctive Russian school of art are to be traced. Nearly all the work is marked by the spirit of the Revival, for the more austere aspects of mid-Byzantine art were never wholly acceptable to the Russian outlook, and from the very first a movement towards tenderness and humanism and away from severity is to be observed as one of the most characteristic features of budding Russian art. It is apparent for instance in the group of portraits of Vladimir's family in Hagia Sophia at Kiev; though painted at much the same time that the mosaics were executed, they are in a far more delicate, more personal style, even allowing for the differences between more or less secular and wholly ecclesiastical subject matter.

We can trace the progress of this movement if the mosaics that adorned the church of the Monastery of St Michael at Kiev, dating from around the year 1108 are compared with those done some 60 years earlier in the Cathedral of Hagia Sophia in the same city. The Hagia Sophia mosaics are in the main to be attributed to Byzantine craftsmen, and are wholly in the monumental style typical of the Second Golden Age of Byzantine art; those of St Michael's church are less rigid as regards the movement of the compositions, while the figures are more personal, their expressions more intimate and tender, and the comprehension more flowing. The work is not perhaps as masterly from the technical point of view as that in Hagia Sophia, but the handling is more sympathetic and a good deal less austere. Each of the apostles in the scene where they are given the bread and wine of the *Communion* by Christ is thus a distinctive personality, and so are the individual saints like St Demetrius, whose mosaic we reproduce (Plate 127). He may be more boorish than are the figures in Hagia Sophia, but he is also more characterful and

XXV Reverse of a
double-sided icon; the
Annunciation; c. 1340.
Macedonian State
Collections, Skopolje.

personal. An angel who occupies a place in the sky in the scene of the *Communion of the Apostles* is more elegant and delicate; he is closely akin to that on the famous icon known as the *Golden Headed Angel* in the Russian Museum at Leningrad, one of the finest products of the twelfth century that have come down to us, whether it is in east or west (Plate XXI). Neither, it is true, have perhaps gone quite as far along the road towards humanism as the figures in the composition of the *Last Judgement* at Vladimir of 1194 (Plate 22), but in both a start along the course has clearly been made.

The influence exercised on the development of Russian art by the wall paintings at Vladimir was very considerable. As we have already seen, they served as inspiration for work in a more provincial manner at Spas Nereditsa near Novgorod, done some three years later (see pp. 35 f.). The Church there was a fine domed building of Byzantine character, the walls covered with paintings from floor to ceiling and comprising a rich series of scenes; its destruction by the Germans during the Second World War was a major tragedy. The iconography derives from eastern sources, but many of the individual figures, Santa Barbara, for example, are distinctly Russian in appearance and not only indicate that a marked progress had been made towards the development of a local style, but also seem to foreshadow the art that was later to be developed by Theophanes the Greek. The composition of the *Last Judgement* would however appear to have been modelled very closely on that at Vladimir([1]).

The influence of the Vladimir paintings is also to be traced in the Church of the Virgin at Suzdal, done in 1233, and it was no doubt also to the fore in other monuments, which were destroyed as a result of the Mongol invasions just before the middle of the century. Other paintings again are akin to the icon of the *Golden Headed Angel*, which we mentioned above, for example, a full-length rendering of the *Annunciation* on a panel in the Tretyakov Gallery (Plate XXII). It is known as the Ustyug Annunciation, but is nevertheless a work of the Novgorod school. Here the expression of the Virgin is personal and tender, and the gesture of her right hand, with which the vision of the child within her womb is indicated, is reverent and delicate. Though in some ways archaic, in that there is no ornamental background and the figures stand as if in silhouette, the panel shows nevertheless the first hints of a particular blend of the real and the spiritual that was later to become one of the most outstanding characteristics of Russian painting. At times, however, as in the icon known as the *Saviour of the Wrathful Eye*, an expression of extreme austerity dominated; the style of the Revival was here moving along very different channels from those taken at Monreale, or even more, from those followed at Kurbinovo and Kastoria, where a keen sense of drama was to the fore rather than one of divine wrath. And it is distinct again from the course taken at Mileševa and Sopoćani, where monumentality and dignity were dominant. But nonetheless, the Russian work shows the influence of the Revival style, and, like all the other manifestations, owes an outstanding debt to the Byzantine metropolis.

In addition to the features we see here, where intimacy and severity, material and spiritual, are blended, other elements appear in paintings done on Russian soil at this time which represent a foretaste of the manner that was soon to become truly Russian, and they serve to distinguish Russian work from that done in the Byzantine world, narrowly speaking, or in the Balkans. Some of these features are already to be noted in a very fine twelfth century icon depicting St Demetrius of Salonica which came from the Cathedral of Dimitrov, and is now in the Tretyakov Gallery at Moscow (Plate 130). It is to be assigned to the Vladimir-Suzdal

school of icon painting, and is one of the most outstanding examples of early Russian art that have come down to us. The rather egg-shaped face, the sloping shoulders and the great attention given to decorative details both in the costume and in the carpet below the Saint's feet are characteristic in this respect. The same features are also to the fore in another fine icon of the twelfth century which represents the Archangel Michael; it came from the Cathedral of the Dormition at Moscow (Plate 128) ([2]). The decorative detail is here treated with the same attention, the archangel's cloak being adorned with a repeat pattern not unlike a fleur-de-lys; it may be contrasted with the much more classical costume worn by St Michael on the Constantinopolitan icon of rather later date at Pisa (Plate 124), which was mentioned in the previous chapter. Though such decorative details are absent, an icon of St Nicholas may also be noted, for there the Russian features take on a rather different character. The long head and the stressing of rhythmical pattern as made by the saint's fingers or the crosses on his robe are thus all features which were more developed in Russian than in Byzantine or Balkan painting (Plate 129).

These icons were probably painted at Novgorod, and from the middle of the thirteenth century that city became the principal centre for the production both of panels and of frescoes, as a result of the conquest of the whole of southern Russia by the Mongols, for in the areas which were under Mongol overlordship very little art was produced. But there were also other schools in the North; those of Yaroslavl and Pskov were the most important of them. The school of Yaroslavl is represented by a number of icons, more particularly a number of small ones depicting scenes from our Lord's life. There is also a very outstanding icon of the Saviour now in the Tretyakov Gallery at Moscow, as well as one depicting the Virgin shown full length in the 'Orans' position, with a medallion containing an archangel on either side above (Plate 132). It is in a severe, archaic style, while the more tender, intimate aspect of the work of the school is to the fore in an icon known as *Our Lady of Tolga*. This represents the Virgin enthroned with the Child on her knee; both figures are redolent of human sympathy, though they remain nevertheless wholly spiritual.

The most important of the works that are to be assigned to Pskov are some wall-paintings in the church of the Svetogorsk monastery there, dating from 1313. The style is rather harsh and crude, but the figures are both powerful and expressive and represent a development of the manner which we first saw at Staraya Ladoga around 1180, though the work is on the whole more provincial. These same features were carried to a further extreme in fourteenth-century paintings in the Cathedral of the Mother of God and they were also to the fore in the icon paintings of the school; a panel of *Our Lady's Assembly*, now in the Tretyakov Gallery, is typical (Plate 133); the colouring is most unusual, for the ground is darkish green, with harsh white lights, and the throne brilliant red; the effect is to be described as abstract rather than representational; the style is provincial. Indeed, the paintings of Pskov are all characterised by a rather primitive, archaic trend, which was also to the fore there at an earlier date in the wall paintings of the Kirov monastery, dating from 1156; they no doubt exercised an important influence on subsequent developments in the region([3]).

A somewhat similar trend to that which we noted in the paintings of the Svetogorsk monastery at Pskov is to be traced in the frescoes in the church of St Michael in the Skovorod monastery at Novgorod, where the figures are slim and elegant, with small heads; they date from around 1360. This church was, alas, destroyed during the war. But in Novgorodian icon painting, on the other hand, a new manner

XXVI Icon. The *Dormition of the Virgin*; Yaroslavl school; c. 1380. The Tretyakov Gallery, Moscow.

developed, characterised by a love of brilliant colours which produced a somewhat poster-like effect. This type of colouring, where the shades are not blended but set in separate compartments as in an enamel has been described by Onasch under the portmanteau word 'polychromy', for the colours were varied and contrasting, even if not subtly blended. Red, blue and yellow were the essential basic ones, but their complementary shades, green to red, orange to blue and purple to yellow, were almost equally important, and their interplay was believed to be profoundly significant in relation to the spiritual character of the painting; today these contrasting colours appeal to us primarily because of their brilliance and gaiety(4). The nature of this polychrome system is especially well illustrated by the main figures on a fourteenth-century icon of the *Annunciation* in the State Museum for the History of Art at Novgorod (Plate 134). The contrast of the green of the angel's robe with the yellow of his cloak is typical, as is that of the pale red with the brown of the wings, or the red and yellow with the blue of the costume of the small figure below, who represents St Theodore Tiron; the sphere of heaven from which the Holy Spirit proceeds is probably a later repaint. The trend towards humanism is perhaps less to the fore here than in the so-called Ustyug *Annunciation* shown in plate XXII, but the Novgorod icon is nevertheless a thing of great beauty, and of a profoundly spiritual character. Indeed, it serves to illustrate how in the course of some two centuries an esoteric approach developed on Russian soil, for the icon is generally more abstract, more symbolical, than were renderings of the same theme produced in the Greek world or in the Balkans. The conception of the Virgin is thus wholly unworldly; there is no attempt to depict her in a natural pose or spinning as was usual at an earlier date.

Though Novgorodian icon painting was at this time in some instances very conservative, it was nevertheless in that city that the truly Russian style in icon painting was most fully developed, and it was at Novgorod that many of the features that were to distinguish Russian art from Byzantine were most rapidly becoming accentuated. In addition to factors already noted, such as the tall figures, the egg-shaped faces, the very accentuated slope of the shoulders, and the stress on rhythmical movement, the poses of the figures were changing, for they were tending to become less rigid and to adopt more varied stances than in the Byzantine world, while the upper parts of the bodies were often bowed forward. Again, the mountains in Russian icons were invariably much more stylised and more angular than those of the Byzantine ones. But most important of all was the Russian love of abstraction. Even when the theme to be depicted was of a fairly straightforward or representational nature, it was often treated in an abstract manner; an icon of the *Ascent of Elijah to Heaven* is an excellent example of this tendency (Plate 131); painted in north Russia, it represents an imaginative composition of originality and beauty.

Even more characteristic, however, was the growth in popularity from the fourteenth century onwards of icons where the theme itself was abstract. Rublev's rendering of the *Old Testament Trinity* (see p. 175) illustrates this tendency, for the figures are not so much depictions of the three angels entertained by Abraham at the Oak of Mamre as symbols of the Divine Trinity itself (Plate 138). But it is still a more or less representational picture, whereas other icons depict far more complicated and esoteric subjects, such as the 'Ritual of the Feasts' or 'All Creation Rejoiceth in Thee' — a particularly fine example of this theme was at a later date painted by Dionysius and is now in the Tretyakov Gallery. Its colouring and style are typical of the art of Novgorod at this time, even though the icon was painted more than a century later in Moscow.

Though it was in the fifteenth and sixteenth centuries that these features became most marked, they would appear to have reached an advanced degree of development by the second half of the fourteenth century, for many of them are present in frescoes done between 1370 and 1380 in the church of St Theodore Stratelates at Novgorod, usually dated to 1363, in that of the *Dormition* at Volotovo (Plate 139), (destroyed during the war), or in that of the *Saviour* at Kovalevo, painted around 1380([5]). Both at Volotovo and at Kovalevo the work is extremely powerful and expressive, at times even exaggeratedly so, though it is basically profoundly spiritual. Paintings in the Church of the Nativity in the cemetery at Novgorod, which date from the end of the fourteenth century, are in a rather different style, but the figures are alive, the faces characterful, nonetheless. Perhaps the best of all the works of this phase are some later paintings at Vladimir. They are very alive and expressive and at the same time decorative and delightful; a detail of the scene of the *Anastasis* may serve to illustrate their character (Plate 135). They have been attributed by different authorities to Rublev, to one of his pupils, and to Daniel Cheorny, who worked with Rublev and with Theophanes.

A particularly noteworthy feature of all these paintings, especially those at Volotovo, is the way in which the highlights are applied; they take the form of thin parallel lines or harsh dashes in white. The technique had been used in the Byzantine world, but never with quite the same daring effect, though it was a painter from Constantinople who was to develop the mannerism to its fullest extent, namely the man we know as Theophanes the Greek. He is one of the first Byzantine artists to stand out as a personality, even if he is not the first to be known by name. Records show that he worked on a considerable number of wall paintings in Constantinople, but unfortunately nothing survives there that can be definitely assigned to him. It is, however, very probable that his early style was close to that of the man who did the wall paintings in the parecclesion at Kariye Camii around 1315.

Theophanes' frescoes in Russia are, however, very different. There is little of tenderness, nothing of sweetness. Often the proportions are exaggerated, the poses dramatic and the faces severely stylised. Yet the figures are dynamic, and though in colouring he used reflexes in lighter shades of the basic colours with very great skill, and lent to his figures a profoundly spiritual character, his highlights were slashed on with a bravura that has seldom been equalled. As Onasch expresses it (p. 20) with regard to his lighting, he worked on the borderline between the inner luminosity proper to the icon painter and the system of cast light that was normal in the west. In his treatment of light indeed his work was akin to that of another but more famous Greek painter, the great Domenikos Theotokopoulos, better known as el Greco. One wonders if, as with Greco, the very personal manner that characterised Theophanes' work was only fully developed late in his life in the land of his adoption, rather than in his Byzantine homeland.

Theophanes worked on at least five churches in Moscow and on others elsewhere, but most of this work has perished, and the only paintings that survive are in the Church of the Transfiguration at Novgorod, which were done in 1378 (Plate 136). They show a fairly close similarity to those we have already mentioned in the Church of the Dormition at Volotovo, Novgorod, usually dated to 1363 (Plate 139). Most of the leading authorities in Russia are agreed that these paintings are not to be assigned to Theophanes himself, but to another painter working in a closely similar manner, though Alpatov inclines to the belief that Theophanes may have had a hand in them. But Theophanes' individual style seems to have been imitated very freely, and there is a good deal of work which could be attributed to him without any great stretch of the imagination, were there not reliable information to suggest that it should be assigned to others. Such are, for example, some later wall-paintings in the Cathedral of the Dormition at Vladimir, akin to Theophanes' style, though there is evidence available to show that they were done by the painter Daniel Cheorny in 1408 (Plate 141).

The problem of attribution is even more difficult with regard to icons, and here the authorities who have studied the panels at first hand are much at variance. Onasch, in his large volume on icons, includes as certainly by Theophanes, a double-sided icon with the Virgin and Child known as *Our Lady of the Don* on one side (Plate XXIII) and the *Dormition of the Virgin* on the other (Plate 140), as well as an icon of the *Transfiguration*; both are now in the Tretyakov Gallery. Lazarev, on the other hand, regards both panels as school pieces[6]. The rendering of the Virgin is tender, intimate and delicate and is undoubtedly a work of great mastery, but it is in the individual figures of the *Dormition* that Theophanes' particular mannerisms are most obvious, and the enlargements of some figures given by Onasch would seem to leave little doubt regarding Theophanes' authorship of this painting, for the treatment of detail is so very close to that of the Novgorod frescoes. The handling of the figures in the *Transfiguration* is less redolent of Theophanes' personal style. It is indeed close to that of the Kariye frescoes, and if this icon is to be attributed to Theophanes, it is surely to be regarded as an early work done before he developed the more mannered style which is to the fore in the *Dormition*. The figure of Christ on this panel is nevertheless closely akin to that on an icon of the *Pantocrator* in the Cathedral of the Annunciation at Moscow (Plate 123), which Lazarev accepts as an undoubted work of Theophanes and dates to 1405[7]: others have attributed it to Rublev or to Daniel Cheorny, a painter who was closely associated with him. This latter attribution is perhaps the most likely. Lazarev also recognises as by Theophanes two panels depicting the Virgin and St John which, together with one of the Pantocrator, once formed a *Deesis*. Both are of great beauty, especially that of St John, who stands in a very expressive attitude of supplication. Here the face is rendered with something of the same impressionist style as that of the figures in the Novgorod frescoes.

Lazarev also associates with Theophanes a number of other panels in the same cathedral; most important are those depicting the archangels Michael and Gabriel, the apostles Peter and Paul, and St Basil the Great[8]. Here the style is more delicate, more impressionist, and the rather violent handling seen in the Novgorod frescoes or in the details of the icon of the Dormition is absent. The style is in fact close to that of Theophanes' most outstanding pupil, Andrew Rublev, and it may well be that the master, in his later years, adopted something of the intimate, refined manner that was to characterise the work of the greatest of all the Russian painters, peer of the leading masters who worked in Italy or the Netherlands at the time.

The date of Rublev's birth is disputed — some think it took place about 1370, though its six-hundredth anniversary was celebrated in the USSR in 1960 and a number of monographs dedicated to his memory were published around that year[9]. He died about 1425. He spent most of his life as a monk in the Monastery of the Trinity and St Sergius at Zagorsk, not far from Moscow, but the first works that can be attributed to him are wall-paintings in the Cathedral of the Annunciation at Moscow done in 1405, where he worked as the associate of Theophanes the Greek. Around 1408 he was painting in the Cathedral of the Dormition at Vladimir and

125, 126 Icons. (above) The *Archangel Michael*; early fourteenth century. Byzantine Museum, Athens. (opposite) '*Our Lady of Pimen*'; later fourteenth century. The Tretyakov Gallery, Moscow.

127 Kiev, St Michael's
Monastery. Mosaic;
St Demetrius; late
eleventh century.

128 (*above*) Icon. The *Archangel Michael*; from the
Cathedral of the Dormition of the Virgin, Moscow.

129 (*above right*) Icon. *St Nicholas*; Novgorod;
twelfth century. The Tretyakov Gallery, Moscow.

130 (*right*) Icon. *St Demetrius of Salonica*;
twelfth century. The Tretyakov Gallery, Moscow.

131 *(above left) Icon.* The *Ascent of Elijah.* North Russian; sixteenth century. The Tretyakov Gallery, Moscow.

132 *(above right)* Icon. The *Virgin Orans;* Novgorod; thirteenth century. The Tretyakov Gallery, Moscow.

133 *(right)* Icon. *Our Lady's Assembly* (detail); Pskov; fourteenth century. The Tretyakov Gallery, Moscow.

134 Icon. The *Annunciation*. Novgorod; fourteenth
century. State Museum for the History of Art, Novgorod.

135 Vladimir, Cathedral of St Demetrius. Detail from the *Resurrection*; fourteenth century.

136 Novgorod, Church of the Transfiguration. Wall painting; an *angel*; by Theophanes the Greek; c. 1378.

he also worked at Zvenigorod; thereafter most of his work was probably done at Zagorsk. The old polychrome style of Novgorod with its brightly contrasting compartments of colour was, as we have seen, in many ways distinct from the system employed by Theophanes, where the colours were subtly blended. It was along these lines that Rublev's colour system developed. His style is thus closer to that of Constantinople, as exemplified by the Kariye frescoes, than it is to that of the fourteenth-century icon painters of Novgorod, with their poster-like contrasts. There are in his paintings no hints of the primitive, provincial elements that we see in the icons done at Pskov or in certain of the other northern cities of Russia. Rublev's system of lighting was extremely subtle, extremely delicate; more so, perhaps, than that of Theophanes. Like Theophanes, he laid stress on the spiritual side of art, by depending on the inner luminosity of the figures which had been so important in earlier work, but he also paid attention to the role of cast light emanating from natural sources.

How much the supreme beauty of Rublev's icons is to be attributed to the influence of new systems of lighting and composition which were developing at the time, and how much to his own personal genius, it is hard to say. He certainly owed a considerable debt to Theophanes, yet his style was individual and he lent to his renderings a new touch of reverential humility which he shares with a man who was in many ways his western counterpart, Fra Angelico. It is recorded that Fra Angelico began his paintings with prayer and the same was no doubt true of Rublev; all his work is redolent not only of spirituality but also of a profound faith, and even in the Byzantine world, where art and the Christian faith were virtually synonymous, he stands out in this respect.

His *Old Testament Trinity* in the Tretyakov Gallery at Moscow is his best known work (Plate 138). It was painted for the Monastery of the Trinity and St Sergius around 1411, in memory of the founder of the monastery, St Sergius of Radonez, who died in 1392, and it has been suggested that, like St Sergius's teaching, it was intended as an assertion of the sanctity of the Trinity, doubts regarding which had arisen at the time. The icon depicts three figures, prosaically the three angels entertained by Abraham and Sarah as recorded in the book of Genesis, chapter 18, verses 1–3, though none of the subsidiary details of the Old Testament scene – Abraham, Sarah, their house, the oak tree, or the feast – are included. But the subject is in reality more profound, for the three figures represented are those of the divine conception of the Trinity, God the Father, God the Son and God the Holy Spirit – a mystic comprehension far removed from anything that was attempted in the paintings of Old Byzantium. It was surely not so much because of the Russian love of rhythm, but rather on the grounds of symbolism that Rublev's composition was based on a series of equilateral triangles.

One would naturally have expected the central figure of this panel to represent the Almighty, but Lazarev has suggested that God the Father is actually that to the left, a figure of great sublimity and grandeur[10]. His identification of the central one as Christ is in keeping with the theological outlook of the day, for it was an age in which stress was laid on the sanctity and power of Christ, while the New Testament was preferred to the Old.

Such esoteric ideas are rather less predominant in panels which form a *Deesis* flanked by Angels which came from Zvenigorod[11] – those of the Saviour and an archangel are the finest of them (Plate 137). The thin, delicate face of the Saviour is in some ways akin to that of the *Deesis* mosaic at Kariye, but the face is thinner and longer, the neck fuller, the shoulders more sloping, and the whole conception is Russian rather than Greek. Notably distinct is the exaggeratedly long nose, which forms the basis of the thin oval face, just as in the Byzantine world a shorter nose served as the radius of the rounder, plumper face; twice this length delimited the outline of the head, and three times the length that of the surrounding halo[12]. Both here and in the Trinity the strange, diaphanous colours are of outstanding beauty. Nowhere, however, is the colouring of the archangel in the Zvenigorod iconostasis surpassed. Here the ochre of the angels' wings, the blue of the feathers and the pinkish-red of the garments are not only wholly unexpected, but also profoundly effective.

These strangely etherial paintings of Rublev's represent the acme of spiritual art. No contemporary painter was able to produce work of quite the same quality, and most of the Muscovite icons executed from the second quarter of the fifteenth century onwards were characterised by a more straightforward approach. Indeed as the century progressed, an almost picturesque style was developed, and it soon became typical of the city which was now both the capital of the country and the main centre of patronage. And with the conquest of Constantinople by the Turks in 1453 Moscow became the chief centre of Orthodoxy also, and as such assumed the role of the 'third Rome'. This new style was to the fore in the wall-paintings in the Cathedral of the Annunciation in the Kremlin, done in 1405, but the true Muscovite manner was most fully developed by the painter Dionysius later in the century. Yet Dionysius was in many ways a conservative painter, and he reverted to the old system of polychromy which had been developed at Novgorod more than a century before. His icons thus have something of the simplicity, the brilliance and the effectiveness of posters in contrast to the much more subtle and complicated nature of those by Rublev and Theophanes and their associates.

In spite of Moscow's newly found importance, work nevertheless continued elsewhere, and in much of it the characteristic features introduced by Theophanes and developed by Rublev, such as the long heads, the oval faces, the sloping shoulders and the subtle colour reflexes, were to the fore, as for example in an icon representing the *Dormition of the Virgin* from Yaroslavl, now in the Tretyakov Gallery at Moscow (Plate XXVI)[13]. It shows less restraint than Theophanes' rendering of the same theme, but the spiritual atmosphere is no less accentuated, and as one looks back, the debt of both to the Kariye frescoes is quite obvious, in spite of the essentially Russian colouring of the Yaroslavl icon. It is one of the last Russian icons that belong essentially to the Byzantine tradition; thereafter the 'poster' style that passed from Novgorod to Moscow became more and more popular, while new themes and manners were developed which were wholly Russian. Among the panels devoted to new themes, attention may be drawn to the so-called 'founder' icons, where a saint, monk or holy man dominates the picture space, with a view of his monastery behind him. Of the new manners that were developed the most significant is characterised by 'horror vacui'; in icons where this outlook is to the fore every portion of the panel was adorned with detailed decoration, as on those of the so-called Stroganov school. Panels of both types are interesting, often even delightful, but they are not be included in the same category as the glorious spiritual visions of a Rublev or the imaginative conceptions of a Theophanes, and though the basic tradition was still Byzantine, such paintings are hardly to be counted as works of the Byzantine Revival.

7

Paintings of the later fourteenth and fifteenth centuries in Greece and the Balkans

The little town of Mistra in the Peloponnese was founded by the Latins in the middle of the thirteenth century and was conquered by the Turks in 1460; soon thereafter it was deserted. Its life was thus very brief in comparison to that of Constantinople, its appearance equally contrasting; for it is far from the sea and occupies the slopes of a quite considerable mountain. It was ceded by the Latins to Michael Palaeologos in 1259 and around 1350 became the seat of an independent Greek despot who was usually one of the emperor's sons. In a life of hardly two centuries it played a role in the development of Greek thought, even in the revival of classical learning, which was out of all proportion to its size and the duration of its history. It was there that the neo-Platonist George Gemistos Plethon lived and taught, there that the study of ancient Greek philosophy and more especially that of Plato was most intensively pursued, there that the idea of Hellenism was born anew, and thence that the results were carried to Europe and the west, especially by a man who taught there as a philosopher and who afterwards became a Cardinal of the Catholic church in Italy, namely Bessarion. In the west his thinking formed the basis on which much of the philosophy of the Renaissance was to be built up. And though the teaching that Plethon followed was not that of the Byzantine priesthood, so that the church opposed him and his doctrines, Mistra was by no means behind with regard to the development of religious art, and the new impetus that Plethon's teaching lent to the progress of humanism in thought may well have been responsible for the greater humanism of much of the art of Mistra; this was especially so in the paintings of the Pantanassa, which were done around 1428, when Plethon's teaching had had time to make itself felt. Similarly the stress which Plethon laid in his teaching on an ideal unity no doubt led to a desire that art should be sympathetic, clear and logical, as well as in close accord with the thought of the age.

In the earlier work at Mistra, however, there was no occasion for such ideas to make themselves felt, for the first paintings that survive there were executed long before Plethon's birth. They are to be found in the church of St Demetrius, which was founded by Archbishop Nicephoros Moscopoulos of Sparta in 1291. The paintings are to be assigned to two distinct schools, the one conservative, with little attention being given to picturesque elements, backgrounds or details, and the other where the ideas of the Revival were already making themselves felt[1]. The tall figure of the Virgin in the apse is typical of the more conservative work (Plate 143).

Two men, perhaps even two workshops were responsible for that in the more advanced style, one of them working in the south aisle and the other in the main nave, where the Miracles of Christ are depicted in three long friezes. Delvoye compares them to the paintings in the Protaton on Athos. Here the architectural backgrounds are profuse and fantastic, there are numerous figures and they stand in crowded groups, but unfortunately the paintings are in very poor condition today, and it is hard to discern details; drawings made at the time of Millet's visit and published in 1910, give a better idea of their richness and elaboration than any photograph[2].

The next in date of the Mistra monuments is the complex of the Brontocheion, where there are two churches. One is dedicated to St Theodore and was founded around 1290 by Bishop Daniel and finished in 1296 by his successor Pachomios; its paintings are very fragmentary. The other, known as the Aphentiko or Church of the Virgin Hodegetria, was built by Pachomios probably around 1310. It contains the tomb chapel of Theodore I Palaeologos, patron of the monastery, and on the north wall there is a long inscription recording endowments made by Michael VIII (1259–82) and Andronicos II (1282–1328). Above it are painted four angels, supporting a medallion; the medallion has perished, but happily the angels are preserved, for they are of great beauty (Plate 142). In the church itself some very fine paintings remain. There are impressive busts of prophets in the domes – that of Zacharias is especially forceful and dramatic (Plate 146) – and a number of scenes from our Lord's life, which are more intimate and personal, the *Marriage at Cana* and two of Christ's *Miracles* are particularly good (Plate 147). The work is of great delicacy, the touch lighter and more miniature-like than at Constantinople, but nevertheless closely related to what was done at Kariye. The paintings of the Brontocheion are to be assigned to the metropolitan group, the style being quite distinct from that of the realist schools of Salonica and Macedonia which we looked at in a previous chapter.

Another lovely composition in the Church of the Hodegetria appears on the western wall of the southern side chapel – it is a group of martyrs, distinguished by the svelte proportions of the figures and the very lovely colouring of the costumes, in which pinks and reds, deep blues and delicate greens, all blend in an enchanting symphony (Plate 148). Somehow, though lighter and more delicate, the group recalls the choir of angels in Hagia Sophia at Trebizond, also a work of the Metropolitan school, but done roughly half a century earlier.

Better preserved and more complete than the paintings of the Brontocheion are those in the Church of the Perebleptos, executed apparently in the third quarter of the fourteenth century[3]. The building is on a small scale, but its decoration comprised a very extensive series of New Testament scenes; the best preserved work is that on the vaults and roof. In the conch of the apse is the Virgin between two archangels, with the child on her knees; it is an effective and impressive production. The scenes are more intimate, all are picturesque and full of lively detail, and the style is close to that of the miniature painter. The *Entry into Jerusalem*, for instance (Plate XXVIII), is gay and decorative, with a large welcoming crowd in bright costumes in front of the city gates. Here and indeed in all the scenes, there is a considerable originality of treatment, but throughout an atmosphere of serenity pertains and this led Delvoye to suggest that the work was perhaps inspired by Hesychast philosophy (see p. 150). The same outlook is to the fore in the *Nativity*, which is mystical, even abstract, in treatment (Plate XXVII). The essential properties of the scene – the crib, the rocks, the cave – have taken on the character of formal designs

of an almost abstract character, and the light seems to emanate from within rather than to be cast from any natural source, so that the picture becomes almost a divine revelation. This is even truer of the scene of the *Transfiguration*, where the figure of Christ before a mandorla of unusually complicated geometric form is both wholly human and at the same time wholly divine (Plate 144).

The *Last Supper* once again illustrates this contemplative approach (Plate XXIX). The scene is set before an architectural background of unprecedented elaboration, but it is still a spiritual, not a worldly feast. And the same is true of *Thomas's Incredulity* (Plate 150), though perhaps the beauty of the highlights on the costumes of the apostles is the most striking feature here. The placing of Christ's body on the cross is more dynamic and tells by the lively movement of the figures and the rhythm of the composition; the attitudes must, one feels, have been carefully thought out to express the brutishness of the actors in the scene, and the same is true of the *Deposition* (Plate 149). All these scenes are distinguished by a great profusion of picturesque detail, some of it of an almost baroque character, though material aspects are suppressed.

One may still assign the Perebleptos paintings to the Metropolitan school, and the designation of them as Cretan made by some authorities is most confusing. This term was first used by Millet to distinguish a particular iconographical heritage. It was then extended to cover panel painting or work which was of a miniature-like character from the technical point of view. Then the term came to be applied to the paintings found in a number of small churches on the island of Crete, where the work is on a small scale and where the approach is decorative and idealistic rather than realistic. Further it was extended to cover a group of icons done in Crete, in Venice, and on the mainland of Greece in the sixteenth century. Thus the term 'Cretan' has many diverse meanings and would be better discarded unless it be used in a geographical sense, to apply to the type of painting to be found in most of the churches on the island of that name.

It is equally confusing and equally wrong to apply the term Macedonian to the paintings in the next of the Mistra churches, the Pantanassa, as was suggested by Millet on the basis of certain of the iconographical features that characterise them. There may, among the paintings of the Pantanassa, be certain iconographical features akin to those which distinguished the paintings of Macedonia, Salonica and elsewhere which we examined in a previous chapter—the man who holds his garment to his nose, in the rendering of the *Raising of Lazarus*, to indicate the fact that the corpse was already decomposing may serve as an example of the realism favoured by Macedonian painters. Again, the paintings may be more dramatic than are those of the Perebleptos; but so far as style, colouring and general character are concerned, the paintings of the Pantanassa represent a straightforward development from those of the earlier churches at Mistra, inspired to some extent by changes in thought that had affected the life of the city by the time that they were executed around the year 1428. This is clearly seen if the portraits of the Fathers of the Church or the Saints are compared with the prophets in the Brontocheon (Plates 145 and 146).

The Church of the Pantanassa had actually been founded by the Despot Manuel in 1350, but it was restored and dedicated as a thank-offering to the Virgin by Johannes Frangopoulos in 1428, and its paintings are to be assigned to this restoration[4]. Inside the church is virtually two-storeyed, that is to say, there is a gallery extending over the side aisles and across the western end, and its roof is at the same level as that of the main aisle, itself a barrel vault. In the apse are the

XXVIII Mistra, Greece; Church of the Perebleptos. The *Entry into Jerusalem*; c. 1350.

XXIX Mistra, Greece; Church of the Perebleptos. The *Last Supper*; c. 1350.

Virgin and Child, surrounded by Saints and Prophets – an unusually complex arrangement; on the vault immediately to the west is the *Ascension* (Plate 152), Christ before a mandorla at the centre, with Apostles, the Virgin and an angel below, gazing into the sky with a wooded landscape behind them. Further to the west is the *Entry into Jerusalem* (Plate XXXI). As in the Perebleptos, there is a mass of detail throughout and the scene is redolent of the joy and gaiety of the occasion. A more heavenly joy dominates in the rendering of the *Annunciation*, where the angel appears as if levitated in front of the Virgin (Plate 154). Both are figures of great beauty and profound spirituality, which is enhanced rather than diminished by the detail of a partridge drinking at a little fountain in the foreground. This is a painting of quite outstanding quality, and tells the story with great feeling and particular charm. The delicate poses and enchanting yet strange colours of the scene of the *Presentation* are no less effective (Plate 153). But it is in the scene of the *Raising of Lazarus* that the acme of these paintings is reached; the strange pinks, reds and buffs of the colouring are used with surprising effect and the drama of the event has seldom been more effectively rendered in art (Plates XXX and 151). The feeling, the style and, above all, the colouring of these paintings are quite distinct from anything that is to be found in the north, even if there are iconographical parallels with Macedonian works.

Lazarev, Diehl and others have pointed out that Millet was perhaps too much guided by purely iconographical data in his distinction of the schools. He hardly took style and colouring into account. As study has progressed, we have come to realise that these factors also have a very important role to play, and in the paintings of the Pantanassa the style that characterises the work is certainly nothing like that which dominated in Macedonia. Nor is its nature to be explained as the result of Italian influence, as certain other authorities have suggested. Rather should one regard these remarkable paintings as the result of the effects exercised by the philosophical teachings of George Gemistos Plethon and his colleagues on the artistic heritage that came down from Constantinople. And the nature of that heritage becomes clearer if we look at some of the individual figures like the prophets in the small domes which roof the side aisles at the gallery level, or the figures of the apostles on the walls (Plates 156 and 157). Their curious swaying poses are closely similar to those of the military saints in the parecclesion at Kariye, but the highlights on the faces and costumes are used with an entirely new freedom, though the basic conception of the art remains wholly spiritual, with little hint of the new material or naturalistic outlook which was by 1428 growing up in the west.

Apart from those at Mistra, the finest paintings in Greece are probably to be found in the church known as Omorphi Ecclesia near Athens; they are in poor condition. The few scenes that are well preserved are in a rather forceful, realist style, closer to that of Salonica than to the more polished manner which we associate with Constantinople; they seem coarse and crude in comparison with the work at Mistra. Elsewhere painting in Greece in the fourteenth and earlier fifteenth centuries is nearly all very provincial in character and its interest is primarily local. The same is also true of the wall-paintings that survive in Crete in spite of the considerable fame of the island as a centre of painting and the widespread use of the adjective 'Cretan', which, as we have shown, is open to a great many different interpretations. So far as the wall-paintings of the island are concerned, the term has reference to work in a miniature-like technique and on a small scale, wherein red and blue are the predominating colours. The decoration of the Church of

Valsamonero in the mountains some miles to the west of the Heraklion – Phaistos road are typical and are among the best. They belong to the first half of the fourteenth century. Work at Kritsa further towards the east of the island is in a distinct, more monumental style and is more impressive, though less delicate([5]). The style and the colouring of the paintings of the former group was revived at a later date in the work of the icon painters, especially that of George Klotzas (1564–1609); it is well represented in his icon of the theme 'In Thee Rejoiceth', now in the Greek Institute at Venice([6]).

An approach somewhat similar to that which dominated at Mistra characterises the work of the last phase of painting in Serbia, which had its home in a number of monasteries in the Morava valley. Though the later years of the thirteenth and earlier ones of the fourteenth century, to which period these paintings belong, were by no means happy for Serbia, in that there were constant wars and troubles in face of the Turkish advance into Europe, which steadily progressed after the disastrous defeat of the Serbians at Kossovo in 1389, the art of the age is curiously delicate and tranquil. The liveliness of the paintings of Lesnovo, the expressiveness of those at Marko, are wholly absent in the work of the Morava school; instead we find a calm, other-worldly atmosphere and an art that is placid and contemplative. It seems somehow very much out of the context of its age. Perhaps it was the effect of an escapist mentality; perhaps the character of the principal patron, the Despot Stephen, was responsible, for he was himself a poet and he made of the Monastery of Manasija a centre of thought, writing and learning; or perhaps the teaching of the Hesychast philosophy, which was flourishing on Athos and in Greece at the time, also exercised an effect here, for it advocated salvation by way of contemplation and visionary experience([7]).

The earliest of the Morava valley paintings are those at Ravanića, founded in 1371 as a burial place for Prince Lazar. They were signed by the painter Constantine around 1376. The painting of the *Healing of a Blind Man* may serve as an example of the work there (Plate 155). Ljubostinja was decorated twenty years or so later, and Kalenić in the early years of the fifteenth century, under the patronage of a feudal lord called Bogdan, his wife Milica and her brother Peter. In all of these places the figures are tall and elegant, the faces youthful, the subsidiary features decorative and delightful. All these factors are apparent in the depiction of the *Marriage Feast at Cana* at Kalenić (Plate XXXII), a beautiful and at the same time an effective picture. The rendering of *The Flight into Egypt* is equally delightful (Plate 158).

At Rudenica the paintings done between 1403 and 1410, are similar, though not probably by the same hand. At Manasija, also sometimes known as Resava, the extreme of elegant delicacy is reached, as in the depiction of *The Vision of St Peter of Alexandria* or the head of the *Archangel Michael* (Plates 159 and 160). The work was executed at Manasija for the Despot Stephen between 1407 and 1418; it represents the last extensive and important decoration to be done in Yugoslavia.

In all these paintings the old love of drama and action has entirely disappeared, and the whole approach is static, meditative, even placid. But there are distinct hints of the style that was to the fore at Constantinople early in the fourteenth century, and the work of the Morava school would seem to have been derived directly from that of the capital. It is thus hard to accept any suggestion that painters from Salonica, where a more vigorous dramatic style would seem still to have been in favour, could have been in any way responsible. But in addition to the elements derived from Byzantium it is possible that Slav ideas exercised an in-

XXX Mistra, Greece;
Church of the
Pantanassa. Detail of
the *Raising of
Lazarus*; 1428.

XXXI Mistra, Greece;
Church of the
Pantanassa. The *Entry
into Jerusalem*; 1428.

fluence, for there are certain similarities between the paintings of the Morava school and those produced in various centres in Russia at much the same time, so that the style of the work cannot perhaps be attributed to Constantinople alone; the intensely spiritual atmosphere is the most important of them.

Though the icons that were produced from the fifteenth century onwards in Russia are better known and on the whole perhaps of higher quality than those painted in the Greek world, some important work was nevertheless done both in Greece itself and in the neighbouring islands which had by that time fallen under the control of Venice. Many of the painters owed a considerable debt to the art of Byzantine Constantinople, even if they never had any actual contact with the city. The icons of the so-called Cretan school were in fact directly dependent on developments at the capital, and the panel painters working in Crete itself, on the Greek mainland, and even in Venice were the most important exponents of the metropolitan style from the beginning of the fifteenth century onwards. Their work is to be seen not only in the museums, monasteries and private collections of Greece, but also at Ravenna and more especially in the large collection in the Church of San Giorgio dei Greci at Venice. An icon of the Prophet Elias in the Byzantine Museum at Athens may serve to illustrate the manner (Plate 163). It is in many ways very archaic, for it was produced in the sixteenth century, though at a first glance one would tend to date it to the fourteenth.

Many of the painters of this age signed their icons; the names of Michael Damaskenos, Victor, Zanfurnari or Theodore Poulakis may be noted amongst many others. Their work is much sought after in Greece today and is just beginning to become popular in the west, and authentic icons by these men fetch high prices. Of them many are fine, all are sincere, but it cannot be claimed that they are all of the same outstanding significance in the story of art as the works of the fourteenth and earlier centuries. Michael Damaskenos was perhaps the most outstanding of these later painters, and his work combines a considerable grandeur of manner with a real feeling for decoration. Some of his best paintings are to be found in the Cathedral at Heraklion in Crete. The Greeks, with some stretch of the imagination, like to call him the friend and youthful companion of Greco. The work of the other men tended to be more purely decorative and the details of the scenes were often quite baroque. But basically their style owed much more to the grand tradition of Constantinople than to the west, though whether this heritage was direct or came by way of Mistra it is hard to say.

In so far as icons depicting Christ, the Virgin or individual saints were concerned the greatest conservatism reigned, for they were sacred images, possessed indirectly of the same miraculous powers as were associated with the figures they represented and with the prototypes that they followed. The types remained constant, the forms regulated by tradition, and it is mainly through technical details that the later work can be distinguished from the earlier. In the case of icons concerned with scenes which were didactic rather than devotional in character, innovations, many of them of a western character, were more frequently introduced as time went on, and quite a number of scenes proper to western iconography began to appear even before the fifteenth century; that of the *Noli me Tangere* which forms the theme of quite a number of good fifteenth and sixteenth century icons affords a case in point. And, in addition to developments of a purely technical character like the use of the minute highlights, hatched in in thin parallel lines, which help to distinguish later work, there were innovations of a wholly baroque character, so that ornate thrones, cherubs and other western features found their way into the art. Often the

icons on which these features are to be seen are both charming and decorative; but they must nevertheless be classed as decadent, for it was not a new art that was being created; rather the effects were produced by the mixing of two older elements, the one Byzantine, the other Italian.

Later work on a larger scale was seldom as good as that on a small, and the wall-paintings that were set up in the smaller churches of Greece and the Balkans in the later fifteenth and sixteenth centuries — large buildings were not normally permitted after the Turkish conquests — are not usually very outstanding. Better and in some cases even really fine work is, however, to be found in some of the monasteries of Mount Athos. The monasteries were comparatively rich; no restrictions were imposed there by the Turks as to the size of the churches that could be built, and consequently the decorations were full and elaborate. It was there that most of the more important painters found an opportunity to work, and in the sixteenth century there was a phase of very considerable activity. The main church in the Monastery of the Lavra was thus decorated by a man called Theophanes in 1535, the Chapel of St Nicholas there in 1560 and the Refectory between 1527 and 1535; the Church at Dionysiou was adorned in 1547, that at Dochiariou in 1568, the chapel of St George in the monastery of St Paul in 1555, and the old church of Xenophontos between 1544 and 1563. There is interesting work to be seen in all these places, some of it strikingly modern in its appeal.

In very many cases the scenes have an admirable decorative quality; the *Transfiguration* at the Lavra, for example, is not only a well balanced, well composed picture; in addition, the painter has obviously taken great delight in the decorative character of the mandorla behind our Lord and the angular patterns of the rocks (Plate 162). Again, the individual figures often show great character, particularly those of a subsidiary nature, where the artist could exercise his imagination, unfettered by ecclesiastical conventions; the servant in the scene of *Christ at Emmaus* affords a striking example (Plate 161); he has a strangely expressive face, with a mass of red hair piled up on the top of his head. More individual than the paintings of the Lavra are those in the old church of the Monastery of Xenophontos. Two painters worked there. One of them, called Theophanes, depicted certain scenes in 1563. (He was not the same as the Theophanes who painted in the church of the Lavra.) The other was a certain Anthony, who decorated the nave in 1544, and he seems to have developed a very personal style which though in many ways inept nevertheless succeeded, more than that of any other painter, in achieving a strange unworldly brilliance. Once more the teachings of Hesychasm were exercising their influence. The effects he achieved were accomplished partly thanks to the rather cold, icy colours he favoured, and partly by a profuse employment of bright highlights, made more intense by the black backgrounds. His very individual style is to the fore in the scene of the *Sleeping Apostles in the Garden*. The daring way in which the highlights are slashed on is equalled only by the wholly abstract forms of his landscapes or the imaginative symbolism with which the glory of heaven is rendered in the *Nativity* (Plate 164); they are balanced by the sweeping lines of the Virgin's couch, and the strange angular convention of the cave in which, according to an apocryphal text which was held in great favour, the birth of Our Lord took place.

It is no great remove from the technique of this painter to that of el Greco, and the differences of date are not considerable, for Greco was born between 1541 and 1550 in Crete and went to Italy about 1561; the Xenophontos paintings were done about 1560. Could Greco have seen them, or was he familiar with something in

Crete that was closely akin? If we compare his painting of St Francis receiving the Stigmata, the probability that Greco had studied works like those of Anthony seems very considerable, for the way in which he used the highlights here and indeed in much of his later work, seems to belong to the same stream of art, to follow the same convention that was developed in the monastery of Xenophontos on Mount Athos — though Greco was of course able to add to this heritage the contribution of his own very individual and outstanding genius. So far as the paintings that survive in the Byzantine world are concerned, however, it was only in this one monastery that this very distinctive mannerism was fully developed in the sixteenth century. There are few, if any, wall paintings in Crete itself that can be compared[8], for nearly all that survive there are either minor works or are of earlier date and are in quite a distinct style, being characterised by a minute manner, by great attention to detail, and by a more restricted palette. And there is little similarity between the paintings of Greco and those of the Cretan icon painters of his age. Only in the work of one other man, Theophanes the Greek, were highlights used in the same daring way. But this man was a Constantinopolitan who went to Russia before 1400.

It is perhaps not possible to cite any absolute evidence to establish the Byzantine origins of Greco's art, but that there were many Byzantine elements in his work is hardly to be denied, for in his later paintings he reverted time and again to Byzantine mannerisms, iconography and ideas. His great canvas *el Espolio*, painted at Toledo between 1577 and 1579, is thus clearly modelled on a Byzantine depiction of the *Kiss of Judas*; the *Death of Count Orgas*, done at Toledo in 1586, makes use of the death theme hallowed in the Byzantine world by centuries of usage, both for the *Dormition of the Virgin* and for the death of an ascetic like St Ephraim the Syrian; in the *Adoration of the Name of Jesus* the heavenly and mundane worlds are united in a wholly Byzantine fashion.

In a less concrete direction the way in which a cold light is used to dematerialise form in the *Martyrdom of St Maurice* is a Byzantine mannerism, even if, as Miss Hadermann-Misguich notes, Greco here draws his highlights from a single source, whereas in Byzantine painting the sources are multiple. Byzantine again are technical tricks, such as the intensive use of highlights or the habit of conceiving scenes in verticality rather than in depth, which reaches its fullest degree in the late *Assumption* at Toledo or the *Resurrection of Christ* in the Prado; in both these paintings the lack of attention that is paid to material space belongs essentially to a Byzantine rather than to a western outlook, even though the iconography of both scenes is wholly western. In his depictions of Christ, Greco once more well-nigh invariably sets Him before a reflex of colour, clearly derived from the idea of the mandorla or halo of glory indicated in Byzantine art in a more material form in such scenes as the *Transfiguration* or the *Ascension*. Further, in order to intensify the spiritual aspect of the picture he illuminates his figures with a light that seems to emanate from within rather than to be cast from some natural source, as was usual in the west. Figures other than that of Christ are also at times backed by masses of shade which give the effect of a mandorla in negative; they recall the couch or bed on which the Virgin lies in a Nativity scene or the mouth of the cave in which the event takes place according to the favoured apocryphal variant; we see such a rendering in the Perebleptos at Mistra, and it may be aptly compared. Finally Greco's painting of Toledo, in the Casa Greco there — sadly faded alas by the sun — may be cited. In it the Tavera hospital, invisible from the standpoint which he assumed when painting his view, has been wafted into the centre of his painting on a cloud, just as the saints or the elect are shown on clouds in a Byzantine painting of the *Last Judgement*. No one but Greco in the west would, around 1600, have so flagrantly disregarded the dictates of the actual. To the Byzantine mind, nurtured on the miraculous, this was nothing exceptional. Nor were the strange proportions of Greco's figures without parallel there. 'Learn, o my pupil' wrote the monk Denys of Fourna in the famous *Painters' Guide*, 'that the body of a man is nine heads in height'. Actually it is seven, but Denys' proportions had prevailed in the Byzantine world for many centuries, and much in Greco that the ignorant have sought to explain by astigmatism is made clear by this injunction. So, and in other ways too, can we account for his moving conception of the Laocoon. As my friend Robert Byron once wrote, 'A dubious posterity has thought to discern an astigmatism in his eye. Let it grieve also that same astigmatism which for thirty generations afflicted the artists of Byzantium; the astigmatism of fixation on reality. Are we not too after four centuries again infected?'.[9]

The question of Greco's Byzantinism cannot be left without some reference to the lovely Modena triptych (Plate 165).[10] Its three leaves are all painted on both sides, so that it comprises six paintings in all. Its form is one that was not very usual in Italy, though it was common enough in the Byzantine world. There indeed even more elaborate variants were usual in the sixteenth century, for not only were both sides of the leaves painted, but the central panel often formed the basis for independent leaves on both its faces, so that there are no less than ten painted faces; an example with six faces was shown at the Byzantine exhibition in Athens in 1964, and there is a fine one with ten painted sides in Lord Crawford's collection at Balcarres.[11]

The subjects that are depicted on the leaves of the Modena triptych are of varied provenance, and it would seem certain that the painter used engravings as models for some at least of his compositions. The panel of Christ crowning a military saint was based on counter-reformationist woodcuts, while other compositions owed a debt to Dürer, and others to Titian.[12] It was at one time suggested that the view of Sinai was also modelled on a woodcut published in Poland and dated 1668.[13] This may have been the case, but even so, the ultimate Byzantine origin of the theme cannot be disputed; a view which is wellnigh identical appears on an icon of the sixteenth century owned by Mr Wilfred Blunt (Plate 166) and there is another view of Sinai on an icon in the Vatican.[14] Further, the way in which the mountain peaks are depicted goes back to much earlier prototypes, for the very same mountains appear as the background to the rendering of the scene of the *Transfiguration* in Byzantine art at least from the twelfth century onwards; a very beautiful page in a manuscript in the Bibliothèque Nationale dated to between 1370 and 1375 may be cited (Plate 167).

The Modena panel is signed in the manner usual among icon painters, χειϱ λ ομηνιχου – later, when he got to Spain, Greco more often substituted for this another formula, writing after his name the word ἐπόει, 'made it'; sometimes he added the designation 'κϱής', 'The Cretan'. But he signs χειϱ η ομηνιχου on some of his later paintings, for example that of the *Magdalene* at Worcester, Mass., so that the Modena signature is not unique; it is certainly not to be regarded in itself as adequate evidence for assigning the paintings to another hand as Wethey proposes. He believes that both the Modena triptych and the painting of Sinai formerly in the Hatvany collection at Budapest were the work of a wholly different painter also named Domenikos[15]. It stands to reason that every man who signed 'The hand of Domenikos' was not necessarily the man we know as el Greco; if the signatures are genuine, two rather second-rate icons in the Benaki collection at Athens which bear this name serve to prove the point, for they cannot conceivably be by the man who later worked in Spain. But the Modena triptych is of such high quality and attests so marked a genius in its painter that it is tempting to dispute Mr Wethey's conclusion in its case; and if the Modena triptych is indeed by Greco, it serves as another important pointer to his Byzantine origins.

That Greco, born in Crete, moved quite early in his life from there to Venice is, of course, in no way surprising. Crete was a Venetian possession, and there was a large Greek colony in Venice, numbering many icon painters amongst its members, and it was there that the majority of the most important of them worked, in any case for a part of their lives. These men retained their Byzantine style; Greco, during his Italian period, almost wholly forsook it. But, arrived in Spain, he returned to it with increasing enthusiasm, so that his later work shows similarities to the Byzantine, not only in details of iconography, but in numerous mannerisms also. But it is not so much with regard to a multiplication of individual instances that the debt is to be estimated; rather it is to be traced in the deep-seated similarity of his conception of the spiritual world to that prevalent in Byzantine art, and more especially to that of painters whose outlook owed a debt to the mystic conceptions of Hesychast thought. Greco was above all a mystic; the earlier Byzantine artists and thinkers were not mystics; they were, rather, ascetics, whose efforts to attain to the spiritual world were assisted by the mortification of the flesh rather than by any mental exercise aimed at dissociating them from it.

The earlier Byzantine forms in art thus remained firm and solid, however much they depended on rhythm and however much they sought the spiritual. In Greco's work there was a new dynamism, a new love of swirling movement which lifts the figures of the painting and the minds of the spectators alike into a wholly distinct spiritual world, in a way which few other painters have been able to accomplish. Yet the progress towards that accomplishment was a feature of the Byzantine Revival and, had it not been for the earlier developments of the Revival style which we have been examining, the realisation might never have been possible. The achievement of the spiritual was one of the normal objectives of Byzantine art; as Bréhier put it, the very purpose of that art was to render visible the mysteries of the supernatural world for the benefit of the believer. Art, having the same sacramental character and set form as the liturgy, had the supreme purpose of presenting to the believer all the truths which he had to accept and all the divine and saintly beings whom he had to contact through communion and prayer.[16] Many of the exponents of this art in the phases before 1453 succeeded to a greater or lesser degree in accomplishing this aim – Rublev and Theophanes the Greek in Russia, the men who worked in the Pantanassa and the Perebleptos at Mistra, the masters of Kariye, Sopoćani, Mileševa or Nerez in Yugoslavia, those who worked in Hagia Sophia at Trebizond, the man who painted the icon *Our Lady of Vladimir* and perhaps foremost of all, the mosaicist who wrought the *Deesis* panel in Hagia Sophia at Constantinople. All were Greco's forerunners and in this respect, if in no other, in the spiritual, unworldly, yet wholly human character of his art, Greco may still be considered the last of the Byzantines.

138 Icon. The *Old Testament Trinity*; by Andrew Rublev; 1411.

139 *(above)* Volotovo, near Novgorod. Wall painting; head of *Abraham*; 1370–80.

140 *(above right)* Icon. The *Dormition of the Virgin*; probably by Theophanes the Greek; end of the fourteenth century. The Tretyakov Gallery, Moscow.

141 Vladimir, Cathedral of the Dormition. *Head of Abraham*, by Daniel Cheorny; 1408.

142, 143 Mistra, Greece. Monastery of the Brontocheon,
Church of the Hodegetria. *Angels supporting a medallion*;
c. 1300. *(above left)* Church of St Demetrius. *Virgin*, in
the apse; c. 1300.

144 *(right)* Mistra, Greece; Church of the Perebleptos.
The *Transfiguration*; detail of *Christ*; c. 1350

145 (*right*) Mistra, Greece; Church of the Pantanassa. A *saint*; 1428.

146 (*below right*) Mistra, Greece; Monastery of the Brontocheon. The *Prophet Zacharias*; early fourteenth century.

149, 150 *(opposite)* Mistra Greece; Church of the Perebleptos. c. 1350. *(above)* The *Deposition*; *(opposite below)* the *Incredulity of Thomas*.

147, 148 Mistra, Greece; Monastery of the Brontocheon. Wall paintings; early fourteenth century. *(right) Healing of the Blind Man*; *(below) Martyrs*, at the west end of the north aisle.

151 Mistra, Greece; Church of the Pantanassa. The *Raising of Lazarus*; 1428.

152, 153, 154 Mistra, Greece; Church of the Pantanassa; 1428. *(top right)* Part of the scene of the *Ascension of Christ. (below right)* the *Presentation in the Temple; (centre right)* the *Annunciation.*

ХСНСЦѢЛѤНЖЕѠРОЖЕНІАСЛѢПАГО

158 *(above)* Monastery of Kalenić, Serbia. The *Flight into Egypt*; c. 1400.

155 *(opposite above)* Monastery of Ravaniča, Serbia. *Healing of the Blind Man*.

156, 157 *(opposite below)* Mistra, Greece; Church of the Pantanassa. *Apostles*; 1428.

159, 160 Monastery of Manasija (Resava), Serbia *(left)* View of *St Peter of Alexandria;* 1407–18. *(right)* The *Archangel Michael.*

161 *(above)* Monastery of the Lavra, Mount Athos. Detail of the *Last Supper* –
a servant; 1535.

162 *(below)* Monastery of the Lavra, Mount Athos. The *Transfiguration*; 1535.

163 *(above)* Icon.
The *Prophet Elias;*
fourteenth century.
The Byzantine
Museum, Athens.

164 *(above right)*
Monastery of Xeno-
phontos, Mount Athos;
Old Church. The
Nativity; c. 1544.

165 Panel; the Mon-
astery of St Catherine
on Mount Sinai. Detail
of the *Modena Triptych*
by el Greco; c. 1562.

166 Icon of the late sixteenth century; the Monastery of St Catherine on Mount Sinai.

167 Manuscript illu-
mination. The *Trans-
figuration*; 170–75.
From the manuscript
of John Cantacuzenos,
Bibliothèque Natio-
nale, Gr. 1242.

Acknowledgement

The author and publishers are grateful to the following for providing photographs:
Alinari, plates 50 and 71; Anderson, plates 20, 21, 68, 72, 73, 74, 75, 76; Anisimov,
plate I; Mr Wilfred Blunt, plate 166; Böhm, plate 121; The Byzantine Exhibition,
Athens 1964, plates 96, 101 and 120; The Byzantine Exhibition, Edinburgh 1958,
plates 92, 94, 95, 124 and XXIV; The Byzantine Institute, plates 7, 100, 102, 111,
113, 114 and 115; The Byzantine Museum, Athens, plates 104, 125 and 163; The
Bulgarian Academy of Sciences, plates 51, 52, 53, 54 and 58; Central Commission
of Ancient Monuments, Belgrade, plate 97; Conservation Department, Belgrade,
plate 32; Conservation Department, Skopolje, plate 91; The Courtauld Institute of
Art, plate 26; Department of Fine Art, Edinburgh University, plate 165; Deutsche
Fotothek Dresden (Grossmann), plates 131, 134, 137, XXI, XXII, XXIII; The
Dumbarton Oaks Collection, plate XVII; Ghasilov, plates 24, 25, 123, 127, 135,
136, 139, 141 and XIII; Ian Graham, plates 5 and XX; P. Geuthner, Paris, plate
59 from Grabar, *La Peinture Religieuse en Bulgarie*; The Hermitage Museum,
Leningrad, plate 103; Hirmer, plates 6, 117, 124, 126, 167 and XXV; Professor
V. N. Lazarev, plates 22 and 122; Dr Ljubinković, plates 30 and 56; Macedonian
Conservation Department, plates 9, 16 and 85; Melitzis, plates 2 and 4; G. Millet,
plates 78, 80, 143, 144 and 161; The National Gallery of Art, Washington, plate 67;
Josephine Powell, plates 1, 8, 10, 11, 12, 13, 14, 15, 17, 18, 19, 29, 32, 33, 34, 35,
36, 37, 39, 40, 41, 42, 43, 44, 45, 46, 49, 55, 69, 70, 82, 83, 84, 86, 87, 89, 90,
100, 105, 107, 108, 109, 110, 111, 112, 147, 148, 149, 151, 153, 154, 155, 158,
159, 160, VI, VII, VIII, IX, X, XI, XIV, XXVII, XXVIII, XXX, XXXI, XXXII;
Photo Rashka, plate 98; The Russel Trust, plates 57, 60, 61, 62, 65, 66, III, IV and
V; Madame Sotiriou, plates 23, 47, 48 and 79; Wim Swaan, plates II, XVIII and XIX,
reproduced from *Constantinople* by David Talbot Rice, by permission of the publishers, Paul Elek Productions Ltd; The Tretyakov Gallery, Moscow, plates 128,
129, 130, 132, 133, 138, 140 and XXVI; The Vatican Library, plate 28; The
Victoria and Albert Museum, London, plate 119; The Walters Art Gallery, Baltimore, plate 27; Professor Xyngopoulos, plates 99, XV and XVI.

Notes

CHAPTER 1

1   The most convenient study is that of E. Diez and
O. Demus, *Byzantine Mosaics in Greece*, Harvard,
1931. An attempt to assign them to around 1000
rather than to the previously accepted date of just
before 1100 has recently been made by A. Frolow;
see 'La date des mosaïques de Daphni', *Revue Archéologique*, 1963, p. 183; this dating has not been
generally accepted and on stylistic grounds it is extremely improbable.
2   See D. Talbot Rice, *The Art of Byzantinum*, London
1959, plate 150. Plate 151 is closely akin to it and is
perhaps to be assigned to the same workshop.
3   Konrad Onasch, *Icons*, London, 1963, p. 341.
4   There is a rather clumsy rendering of the theme on
an ivory of the ninth century in the Walter's Art
Gallery at Baltimore; see *Early Christian and Byzantine Art — an Exhibition held at the Baltimore
Museum of Art*, 1947, No. 160, plate XX.
5   See their *Byzantine Art*, London, 1926, p. 15, where
they write that the manner grows hard and dry before the end of the twelfth century and assert that
the story of Byzantine art ends with the Latin conquest of 1204.
6   T. Whittemore, *The Mosaics of Hagia Sophia at
Istanbul*, IV, Oxford, 1952. C. R. Morey, in *Bulletin
of the Metropolitan Museum, New York*, N.S. No. 2,
1944, p. 204. A. Grabar, *Byzantine Painting*, Skira,
1953, p. 107. V. Lazarev,' Les procédés de la stylisation
linéaire dans la peinture byzantine des X-XIIièmes
siècles et leurs sources', *XXV Congrès international
des Orientalistes*, Moscow, 1960, and *Istoria Byzantiniski Jivopis*, Moscow, 1957, p. 116.
7   G. Galassi, *Roma o Bizanzio*, II, Rome, 1953, p. 320.
O. Demus, 'Die Entstehung des Paläologenstils in der
Malerei', in *Berichte zum XI Internationalen Byzan-
tinisten Kongress*, Munich, 1958, No. IV, 2, p. 16.
S. Bettini, 'I mosaici dell'Atrio di San Marco e il loro
sequito', in *Arte Veneta*, VIII, 1954, pp. 37 f,
I myself wavered at one time; see *The Art of Byzantium*, London, 1959, notes on plates XXV-XXVII. For
a re-estimation of my ideas as to the date and for
notes on other works of the twelfth century revival
see 'The Ivory of the Forty Martyrs at Berlin and
the Art of the Twelfth Century', in *Recueil des

Travaux de l'Institut d'Etudes Byzantines, No. VIII,
Belgrade, 1963, pp. 275 f.
8   D. V. Ainalov, *Byzantine Painting in the XIV century*, Petrograd, 1917 (in Russian).
9   Ainalov's thesis that a love of realism and a conception of the pathetic in Byzantine art emanated
from the West depends on the assumption that these
factors only appeared in the Byzantine world in the
fourteenth century. The existence of works in the
new manner which belong to the twelfth century
wholly invalidates it.
10   K. M. Setton, 'The Byzantine background of the Italian Renaissance' in *Proceedings of the American
Philosophical Society*, Vol. 100, No. 1, Philadelphia,
1956, pp. 33 f.
11   One of the first to realize the importance of the
frescoes at Nerez, apart from Okunev who discovered
them, was P. Muratov, who treated the phase of art
from Nerez to Kariye and beyond as one continuous
development; see *La Peinture byzantine*, Paris, 1928,
pp. 117 f. Though recent research has corrected
certain details and conclusions as to dates, his thesis
was revolutionary in his day, even if his use of the
term 'Neo-Hellenistic' to describe the new art, may
be criticized. For good coloured reproductions of the
Nerez paintings see D. Talbot Rice and S. Radojčić,
Yugoslavia: Mediaeval Frescoes, Unesco, 1955.
12   *Thessalonique et la peinture macédonienne*, Athens,
1955, p. 18.
13   Xyngopoulos notes the presence of the scene of the
Lamentation at Bačkovo, in Bulgaria, at a rather
earlier date than Nerez, and suggests that it was first
developed at Salonica, where it appeared among the
paintings of Kazandjilar Camii, now destroyed.
Another of the paintings at Bačkovo is clearly based
on the mosaic of the Vision of Ezekiel in Hosios
David there; see *Thessalonique et la peinture macédonienne*, p. 17. But this does not necessarily mean
that there was no early rendering of the Lamentation
at Constantinople, for Grabar has noted the Constantinopolitan character of the Bačkovo paintings in
other respects.
14   How very different this work was from that of Italy
is clearly shown if the Nerez paintings are contrasted

with those of 1181 at Castelcastagna, which are very typical of the Romanesque style; see F. Bologna, *Early Italian Painting*, London, 1964, plates 38 and 39. Bologna's otherwise excellent book is hampered by a failure to appreciate the true character of the best twelfth century Byzantine painting and by repeated references to the stale and mechanical nature of the Byzantine court style.

15 J. Milković-Pepek, 'Les motifs delicats de l'art byzantin des Balkans et le problème de la Vierge Pelagonitissa' in *Sbornik of the Archaeological Museum of Skopje*, II, 1958. R. Ljubinhović's article, 'Die alte Kirche in Kurbinovo am Preshasee, *Starinar*, XV, 1940, pp. 100 f., may also be consulted for an account of the paintings as a whole.

16 'Eine spätökomenische Verkündigungsikone des Sinai und die zweite byzantinische Welle des 12. Jahrhunderts' in *Festschrift von Einem*, Berlin, 1965, p. 306.

17 R. Stylianou, 'The wall paintings of the church of the Panaghia tou Arakou at Lagoudhera, Cyprus', in *Proceedings of the IX International Congress of Byzantine Studies at Thessalonica*, 1958, Athens, 19, p. 439 (in modern Greek). See also A. H. S. Megaw, 'Twelfth century Frescoes in Cyprus' in *Actes du XIIe Congrès international des Etudes byzantines*, Belgrade, 1964, Vol. III, p. 261, and A. H. S. Megaw and Ernest Hawkins, 'The church of the Holy Apostles at Perachorio, Cyprus, and its Frescoes', in *Dumbarton Oaks Papers*, XVI, 1962, pp. 277 f.

18 Some authorities have sought to date part of the decoration after 1200. Kitzinger, however, shows that this theory is erroneous and his view that all the work was accomplished during the reign of William II (1171-89), or very soon after, can now surely be accepted; see *The Mosaics of Monreale*, Palermo, 1960, p. 17 and note 2.

19 Two pages from the Paris manuscript are illustrated by Ebersolt, *La Miniature byzantine*, Paris, 1926, plates XXXV (1) and XXXVI. For the Vatican manuscript see C. Stornajolo, *Miniature delle Omilee di Giacomo monaco e dell'Evangelioro Greco Urbinate*, Rome, 1910, and for a fuller discussion of that at Paris, L. Bréhier in *Monuments Piot*, 24, 1921.

20 It was at one time assigned to the eleventh century and regarded as a work of a Greek painter introduced by Abbot Desiderius. Recent research, however, shows that the painting can hardly be dated before the second half of the thirteenth century; see M. Bonicatti, 'Considerazioni su alcumi affreschi medioevali della Campagnia', in *Bolletino d'Arte*, 43, 1958, p. 12.

21 M. G. Sotiriou, 'Les debuts de la Renaissance des Paleologues en Grèce continentale et dans les Isles grecques au XIIIième siècle', in *Deltion of the Christian Archaeological Society*, Part 4, Vol. 4, Athens, 1964, p. 259 (in Greek with a summary in French). She mentions also a number of other decorations in the new style, but of thirteenth century date, which are to be classed as 'metropolitan' rather than provincial, monuments.

22 Igor Grabar, *Die Freskomalerei der Dimitrij Kathedrale in Wladimir*, Berlin, 1927.

23 V. N. Lazarev, '*Old Russian Murals and Mosaics*', Phaidon, 1966, especially p. 128. See also the same author's '*Freski Staroi Ladogi*', Moscow, 1960, and V. K. Miasoedov, '*Freski Spas-Nereditse*,' Leningrad, 1925.

24 See *The Art of Byzantium*, plates 176 and 177, and for a full publication, Stornajolo 'Miniature della Bibbia Cod. Vat. Regin. Gr. 1 e del Salterio Cod. Vat. Palat. Gr. 381', *Collezione Palaeographica Vaticano*, Fasc. II, Milan, 1905.

25 K. M. Setton, 'Byzantium and the Italian Renaissance' *Proceedings of the American Philosophical Society*, Vol. 110, no 1, Philadelphia, 1956, p. 13.

26 Quite a number of scholars from Italy and elsewhere in the West went to Constantinople at this time and obtained copies of classical writings. See Haskins, *The Renaissance of the Twelfth Century*, p. 65; see also Setton, *op. cit.* p. 13.

27 K. Krumbacher, *Geschichte der byzantinischen Literatur*, Burt Franklin reprint, p. 276.

28 A. Tuilier, 'Recherches sur les origines de la Renaissance byzantine au XIIIième siècle' in *Bulletin de l'Association Guillaume Budé*, III, 1955, p. 71.

CHAPTER 2

1 This possibility was first suggested by Miss der Nercessian, in H. R. Willoughby, *The Four Gospels of Karahissar*, Chicago, 1936, p. XXXIX and was followed up by O. Demus, 'Die Entstehung des Paläologenstils' in *Berichte zum XI. Int. Byz. Kongress*, Munich, 1958, p. 18.

2 H. R. Willoughby, *The Rockefeller-McCormick New Testament*, Chicago, 1932, and *The Four Gospels of Karahissar*, Chicago, 1936.

3 Bibliothèque Nationale, *Exposition Byzance et la France Médiévale*, 1958, nos. 47 and 79; the former was taken to France by delegates sent by Michael VIII in 1269.

4 'An unknown Byzantine Manuscript of the thirteenth century' in *The Connoisseur*, April, 1964, p. 218.

5 *Byzantine Art - A European Art*, Athens, 1964, nos. 294, 298 and 299.

6 See K. Weitzmann, 'Constantinopolitan Book Illumination in the period of the Latin conquest' in *Gazette des Beaux Arts*, LXXXIV, 1944, p. 213.

7 For a discussion of these and other signatures; see S. Radojčić, *Les Maitres de l'Ancien Peinture Serbe*, Belgrade, 1955.

8 It was attributed by Miss M. Avery to a Greek artist from Alexandria who perhaps fled to the West to escape the Moslem invaders around 641, 'The Alexan-

drine style at Sta Maria Antiqua' in the *Art Bulletin*, VII, 1925, p. 131.

9 R. Van Marle, *The Development of the Italian Schools of Painting*, the Hague, Vol. I., p. 479, fig. 270.

10 See Radojćić, *Mileševa*, Belgrade, 1963, for full discussion and excellent coloured plates (text in Serbo-Croat, with summary in English); see also D. Talbot Rice and S. Radojćić, *Yugoslavia: Mediaeval Frescoes*, Unesco, 1955.

11 See A. Venturi, *Storia dell'Arte Italiana*, II, Milan, 1902, p. 467, fig. 316.

12 Two hands, working, however, in closely similar styles, are perhaps to be distinguished here. See V. J. Djurić, *Sopoćani*, Belgrade, 1963, for a series of excellent coloured plates (text in Serbo-Croat with summary in English).

13 Work in the western chapel on the north side and that in the prothesis is to be attributed to the thirteenth century, but that of the central chapel is of the seventeenth century. The western chapel on the south side was painted around 1300, the central chapel soon after and the diaconicon late in the thirteenth century, in a light, vivacious manner, that is quite distinct. The paintings of the exo-narthex, now outside, were done between 1338 and 1346 in a somewhat conventional manner.

14 V. J. Djurić, 'Fresques médiévals à Chilandar', in *Actes du XIIe Congrès international d'Etudes byzantines*, III, Belgrade, 1964, p. 59.

15 G. Subotić, 'L'Eglise rupestre de l'archange Michel près de Struga' in *Recueil de Travaux de la Faculté de Philosophie*, Université de Belgrade, Vol. VIII, Pt. 1, Belgrade, 1964, p. 299 and plate 6 (in Serbo-Croat with summary in French).

16 V. J. Djurić, *Icones de Yougoslavie*, Belgrade, 1961, No. 4, plates IV-VI, or S. Radojćić, *Icones de Serbie et de Macedoine*, Belgrade, 1961, plates 11-13.

17 N. G. Sotiriou, 'Les débuts de la Renaissance des Paléologues en Grèce continentale et dans les Isles grecs au XIIIième siècle' in *Deltion of the Christ. Arch. Soc.*, Vol. V, Pt. 4, Athens, 1964, p. 260.

18 L. H. Grondijs, *L'Iconographie byzantine du Crucifié mort sur la Croix*, Brussels, 1947, plate XIX and p. 160.

19 A. Xyngopoulos, *Thessalonique et la peinture macédonienne*, Athens, 1955, p. 35.

20 These monastic paintings have only recently been uncovered; see D. Koco and P. Milković-Pepek, *Manastir*, Skopolje, 1958. There has been some dispute as to the dates, for these authors assign all the paintings to 1271, whereas others prefer to date the more conservative ones to 1095; see R. Ljubinković, 'La Peinture murale en Serbie et en Macédoine, aux XIe et XIIe siècles' in *IX Corsi di Cultura sull'arte ravannate e bizantina*, Ravenna, 1962, p. 436.

21 A. Grabar, *La Peinture religieuse en Bulgarie*, Paris, 1928, pp. 175 f. Others, however, think that the painters may have been Bulgarians schooled in the metropolitian tradition; see P. Muratov, *La Peinture byzantine*, Paris, 1928, p. 126.

22 A. Grabar, *La Peinture*, plates XXXV and XXXVI, and p. 246.

23 D. Talbot Rice and others, *The church of Hagia Sophia at Trebizond*, Edinburgh, 1968.

24 See also A. Grabar, 'Les fresques d'Ivanovo et l'art des Palaeologues', in *Byzantion*, XXV-XXVIII, Fasc. 2., Brussels, 1957, p. 584.

25 The system of association of St Mark with the lion, St Matthew with the angel, St Luke with the bull and St John with the eagle, was not universally accepted in early times, though it had become normal at least by the eleventh century. Dr S. Petković of Belgrade University, however, informs me that the arrangement we see at Trebizond was quite usual in the seventeenth century in Serbia, especially in the work of a painter named Strachina.

26 K. Weitzmann, 'Eine spätökomenische Verkündigungsikone des Sinai' in *Festschrift von Einem*, Berlin, 1965, p. 306.

27 *Art of Byzantium*, no. 173.

28 Authorities have come to very varied conclusions as to the locality in which they were painted. See V. N. Lazarev, 'Constantinopoli e le Scuole nazionali alla luce di nuove scoperte' in *Arte Veneta*, XIII-XIV, 1959, p. 60, figs. 3 and 4. Lazarev agrees that a Sicilian provenance is most likely. There is a good coloured reproduction of one of them in Bologna, *Early Italian Painting*, plate 47.

29 K. Weitzmann, 'The Thirteenth-century Crusader Icons of Mount Sinai' in *The Art Bulletin*, XLV, Sept. 1963, p. 179. For the manuscripts see H. Buchthal, *Miniature Painting in the Latin Kingdom of Jerusalem*, Oxford, 1957.

CHAPTER 3

1 'Byzantine Art in the West', in *Dumbarton Oaks Papers*, I, 1941, p. 84.

2 For reproduction see A. W. Anthony, *Romanesque Frescoes*, Princeton, 1931, figs. 100 and 101.

3 These paintings were at one time dated to the eleventh century, but recent research now seems to have confirmed the later date; see M. Bonicatti, 'Considerazione su alcuni affreschi medioevali della campania' in *Bolletino d'Arte*, 43, 1958, p. 12.

4 The links between Monreale and Kurbinovo and related paintings in the Byzantine world have recently been stressed by Kitzinger; see *The Mosaics of Monreale*, Palermo, 1960.

5 These crosses have been very fully dealt with by E. Sandberg-Vavala, *La Croce Dipinta Italiana*, Verona, 1929. There are good coloured plates of a few typical examples in F. Bologna, *Early Italian Painting*, London, 1964; see especially plates 20, 21,

22, 41, 42, 43, 44, 67, 68 and 69.

6 An excellent exhibition of panels of these phases was held at Florence in 1937 and most of the exhibits are illustrated in the very full catalogue, *Pittura Italiano del duecuro e trecento*, Florence, 1943. See also an article by Roberto Longhi, 'Guidizio sul ducento, 1939', in *Proporzioni*, II, Florence, 1948, pp. 5 f. The marked stylistic differences between these panels and Byzantine ones becomes especially clear if they are compared with the more or less contemporary works in Russia or those in the monastery of St Catherine on Mount Sinai now being cleaned and examined for the first time.

7 G. de Francovich, 'L'Arte Siriaca e il suo Influsso sulla Pitturo medioevale, nell' Oriente et nell' Occidente', in *Commentari*, II, Florence, 1951; see especially p. 86. His conclusions in the case of Monreale can hardly be accepted in the light of Kitzinger's work, *The Mosaics of Monreale*, Palermo, 1960.

8 R. Valland, *Aquilée et les origines byzantines de la Renaissance*, Paris, 1963.

9 A. H. S. Megaw and S. Stylianou, *Byzantine Painting in Cyprus*, Unesco, 1963; also Megaw, 'Twelfth century Frescoes in Cyprus' in *Actes du XII Con-*

grès int. des Etudes byzantines, III, Belgrade, 1964, figs. 12 and 13.

10 F. Bologna, *Early Italian Painting*, plate 58.

11 See Pietro Toesca, *Pietro Cavallini*, London-Milan, 1960. Most of these scenes are also reproduced by Wilpert, *Die Mosaiken und Malereien*, Birth of the Virgin, p. 924, fig. 438, Annunciation, p. 745, fig. 310; Nativity, p. 755, fig. 320; Presentation, p. 761, fig. 329; Adoration, p. 767, fig. 339 and Dormition, p. 925, fig. 439. The medallion of the Virgin, with St Peter and St Paul, appears on p. 1140, fig. 528.

12 The debt of Giotto to Arnolfo was first fully appreciated by Lazarev; see his *Art of the Protorenaissance*, Moscow, 1956, p. 90 (in Russian).

13 *Studies in Florentine Painting*, New York, 1927, p. 1.

14 E. Carli, *La Peinture sienoise*, Paris, 1955, plate 3 and p. 11.

15 See R. Byron and D. Talbot Rice, *The Birth of Western Painting*, London, 1930.

16 'Duccio and thirteenth century Greek Icons', in the *Burlington Magazine*, LIX, 1931, p. 154.

17 These are figured by F. Bologna, *Early Italian Painting*, plates 62, 63, 64 and 65.

18 V. N. Lazarev, 'Maestro Paolo e la Pittura Veneziana del suo Tempo', in *Arte Veneta*, III, 1954, p. 77.

CHAPTER 4

1 His system of classification, depending as it did mainly on iconography, was criticized at the time by Diehl, 'La dernière renaissance de l'art byzantin' in *Choses et Gens de Byzance*, Paris, 1926, p. 169. He pointed out that on purely iconographical grounds Tintoretto's paintings in the Scuola San Rocca could be classed as Macedonian and Rubens' *Descent from the Cross* as Cretan! The term Macedonian school may stand, though there are many works in the characteristic style to be found outside Macedonia. The term Cretan is wholly unsatisfactory, for it is applied alike to very accomplished and wholly metropolitan paintings like those in the Perebleptos at Mistra and to primitive works of a peasant character in village churches in Crete, to colourful paintings of the sixteenth century in the monasteries of Mount Athos, and to a group of refined and delicate panels often very baroque, many of which were produced in Venice.

2 D. E. Evangelides, *The Virgin of the Coppersmiths*, Salonica, 1954 (in modern Greek).

3 *The Basilica of St Demetrios of Thessalonica*, Athens, 1952 (in modern Greek).

4 See D. Talbot Rice, *Byzantine Art*, Oxford, 1935, plate 13b.

5 A. Procopiou, *The Macedonian question in Byzantine Painting*, Athens, 1962, p. 18. The scenes from the Protation and the church of St Clement at Ochrid which he juxtaposes to support this thesis do not support any identity of painters.

6 The paintings of the Protaton have not been republished since their cleaning. The only adequate reproductions of these and other paintings on Athos still remain those in Millet's album, *Monuments de l'Athos: Les Peintures*, Paris, 1927.

7 S. Radojčić, *Les Maîtres de l'ancienne peinture serbe*, Belgrade, 1955.

8 A. Xyngopoulos, *Thessalonique et la peinture macédonienne*, Athens, 1955, p. 36; Prokopiou, *La Question*, p. 18.

9 See A. Xyngopoulos, *ibid*, and Prokopiou, *ibid*, for the Greek opinion, and for the Slav, V. N. Lazarev, 'Painting of the eleventh and twelfth centuries in Macedonia' (in Russian) in *Actes du XIIe Congrès int. des Etudes byzantines*, Belgrade, 1964, Vol. I and 'Complementary Reports' by O. Demus and S. Pelekannides. The fullest study of King Milutin's school as a whole is that of H. Hallensleben, 'Die Malerschule des Königs Milutin', Vol. 5 of *Marburger Abhandlungen zur Geschichte und Kultur Osteuropas*, Giessen, 1963.

10 *The Art of Byzantinum*, plates XL, XLII and XLIII.

11 For illustrations and an account of Yugoslav icon painting see S. Radojčić, *Icones de Serbie et de Macédoine*, Belgrade, 1961. An interesting exhibition was held during the Byzantine congress at Ochrid in 1961, and its catalogue is of lasting value; see V. J. Djurić, *Icones de Yougoslavie*, Belgrade, 1961.

12 'Les motifs délicats de l'art byzantine des Balkans et le problème de la Vierge Pelagonitissa' in *Sbornik*

of the *Archaeological Museum of Skopje*, II, 1958. For the Sinai icon see G. and M. Sotiriou, *Icones du Mount Sinai*, I, Athens, 1956, fig. 235.

13 The scene on one face would appear to be derived from the composition of the fifth-century mosaic in Hosios David at Salonica. See A. Xyngopoulos 'Sur l'icone bilatérale de Poganovo' in *Cahiers Archéologiques*, XIII, Paris, 1962, p. 341.

14 The churches at Verroia await publication; those at Kastoria have been very fully dealt with so far as illustrations are concerned by S. Pelekannides, *Kasto-*

ria, *Byzantine Wall Paintings*, Thessalonica, 1953 (in modern Greek); plates only; a volume of text is expected.

15 A. Xyngopoulos, *The Wall Paintings of St Nicholas Orphanos at Thessalonica*, Athens, 1964. (In modern Greek, with short summary in French; 16 plates in colour and numerous others in half-tone).

16 'Die Byzantinische Malerei des XIV. Jahrhunderts in Griechenland', in *Hellenika*, I, Athens, 1928, pp. 95-113; see especially p. 100.

CHAPTER 5

1 A. H. S. Megaw, 'Recent work of the Byzantine Institute', *Dumbarton Oaks Papers*, No. 17, Washington, 1963, p. 350.

2 The mosaics were first published by T. Shmit in the *Isvestiya of the Russian Archaeological Institute of Constantinople*, XI, 1906. The work of restoring and cleaning the mosaics of the Church and uncovering the paintings of the parecclesion from beneath colour-wash, added when the church became a mosque, was undertaken by the Byzantine Institute of America in the years following the war. The results are described in three superbly illustrated volumes, published in 1966.

3 There seems no reason to question this identification; though Sir Steven Runciman has shown that there are other possible, even if less likely, claimants; see 'The Ladies of the Mongols', in *Festschrift K. I. Amantos*, Athens, 1960.

4 A. Grabar, 'La décoration des coupoles à Kariye Camii et les peintures italiennes du Dugento' in *Jahrbuch der Österreichischen Byzantinischen Gesellschaft*, VI, 1957, pp. 111 f.

5 For a penetrating and extremely interesting discussion of the problem of the Byzantine so-called 'false perspective', see Gervase Mathew, *Byzantine Aesthetics*, London, 1963, especially pp. 31 f.

6 The basic ideas of Hesychasm were first evolved by a monk of the monastery of St John of Studios at Constantinople in the second half of the eleventh century, but were only fully developed by Gregory Palamas, who died around 1360. He was excommunicated by a special synod called in 1345, but received support from John Cantacuzenos and the excommunication was revoked in 1347. Thereafter the teachings of the Hesychasts were widely accepted. In art the belief in the existence of an inner light is apparent at a much earlier date.

7 The work of cleaning has not yet been fully published. For a preliminary report, see P. A. Underwood 'Work of the Byzantine Institute 1957-58', in *Dumbarton Oaks Papers*, XVI, 1960, p. 215.

8 For the mosaics see A. Xyngopoulos, *The mosaic decoration of the Church of the Holy Apostles in Salonica*, Athens, 1953 (in Greek) and K. Kalokyris, 'L'Eglise des Saints Apôtres de Salonique — ses mosaiques', *XI Corsi di Cultura sull' Arte Ravennate e Bizantina*, Ravenna, 1962, pp. 237 f.

9 The paintings were first fully published in Bulgarian with a brief summary in French, by A. Vasiliev, *The Wall Paintings of Ivanovo*, Sofia, 1954. They were discussed again by A. Grabar, 'Les fresques d'Ivanovo et l'art des Palaeologues' in *Byzantion*, XXVI-XXVII, Brussels, 1957, p. 581, and again by Madame Tania Velmens, 'Les fresques d'Ivanovo et la peinture byzantine à la fin du Moyen âge' in *Journal des Savants*, Troisième centenaire, Paris, Jan.-Mars, 1965, p. 386; see also D. Panayotova, *Bulgarian Mural Paintings of the fourteenth century*, Sofia, 1966.

10 The fullest list and most up to date discussion is that of Otto Demus, 'Byzantinische Mosaikminiaturen', in *Phaidros*, III, Vienna, 1957.

11 The church of Gradać was built by Queen Helena of Anjou, wife of King Uroš I, at the end of the thirteenth century. There are numerous Gothic elements in the architecture, but the paintings are basically Byzantine.

12 'New monuments of Byzantine Painting of the XVI century' in *Byzantiniski Vremenik*, IV, 1951, pp. 122 f. with plates (in Russian).

13 For a colour plate of this and other icons see D. Talbot Rice, *The Art of Byzantium*, London, 1959.

14 For further discussion and colour plates of many of these see D. Talbot Rice, *The Art of Byzantium*, London, 1959, or S. Radoćić, *Icones de Serbie et de Macédoine*, Belgrade, 1965.

15 The important collection of icons in this church, most of them post-Byzantine, has been admirably published by Manolis Chatzidakis, *Icones de Saint-Georges des Grecs et la Collection de l'Institut*, Institut Héllenique de Venise, I, 1962.

CHAPTER 6

1 For the most easily accessible reproductions of these paintings see V. N. Lazarev, *Old Russian Murals and Mosaics*, Phaidon Books, 1966.

2 For good colour plates of these two icons see M. Farbman, *Masterpieces of Russian Painting*, London, 1931, plates III and XV respectively — for Our Lady of Tolga see plate IX, and for a detail of the medallion on the Yaroslavl icon of the Virgin Orans see plate XIII.

3 See V. N. Lazarev, 'The Paintings of Pskov' in *A History of Russian Art*, Vol. II, Moscow, 1954, p. 340 (in Russian).

4 For a discussion of this colour symbolism see K. Onasch, *Icons*, London, 1963, notes on p. 24 and p. 356.

5 For the most convenient series of reproductions see M. K. Karger, *Ancient Russian Monumental Painting*, Moscow-Leningrad, 1965 (in Russian); see also *A History of Russian Art*, Moscow, 1954 (in Russian). M. Alpatov has recently suggested that the Volotovo paintings may be as late as 1380, and have been a work of, or have been influenced by, Theophanes; see 'Die Fresken von Volotovo in Nov-

gorod' in *Jahrbuch der Österreichischen Byzantinischen Gesellschaft*, XV, 1966, p. 303.

6 K. Onasch, *Icons*, London, 1963 — German edition, 1961. The Virgin is figured on plates 86 and 87; the Dormition on plates 88, 89 and 90, and the Transfiguration on plates 91, 92 and 93. See also on plates 88, 89 and 90. V. N. Lazarev, *Theophanes the Greek*, Moscow, 1961 (in Russian).

7 V. N. Lazarev, *Theophanes the Greek*, plates 89 and 90; and for the Virgin and St John, plates 91-95.

8 *Loc. cit* plates 98-107.

9 M. Alpatov, *Andrew Rublev*, Moscow, 1959; V. N. Lazarev, *Andrew Rublev*, Moscow, 1960; I. Demina, *The Trinity of Andrew Rublev*, Moscow, 1963. All are in Russian.

10 V. N. Lazarev, 'La Trinité d'André Rublev', in *Gazette des Beaux Arts*, 1959, pp. 282 f.

11 Onasch, *op. cit.* plates 94-97.

12 E. Panofsky, *Meaning in the Visual Arts*, Anchor Books, 1955, p. 79.

13 *Onasch*, op. cit, plate 116, for a reproduction in colour.

CHAPTER 7

1 At one time all the work was dated to around 1310, but the earlier date of the foundation has now been proved; see M. Manousakas, 'La date de l'inscription de l'église de Saint Démetrius à Mistra' in *Delteion of the Christian Archaeological Society*, IV, No. 1, 1959, p. 72 (in modern Greek with summary in French, p. 167); A. Struck, *Mistra, eine mittelalterliche Ruinenstadt*, Vienna and Leipzig, 1910, pp. 79 f., thought that the more conservative paintings were to be dated before 1300; the more progressive ones are probably to be dated to c. 1310. For the most recent summary of the problem see C. Delvoye, 'Mistra' in *Corsi di cultura sull'arte ravennate e bizantina*, Ravenna, 1964, p. 115.

2 The only complete series of reproductions of the Mistra paintings is contained in Millet's album, *Monuments Byzantins de Mistra*, Paris, 1910. Some of the more important paintings are included among the plates of R. Byron and D. Talbot Rice, *The Birth of Western Painting*, London, 1930, and there are a few plates in colour in Panajotis Kanellopoulos, *Mistra*, Munich-Ahrbeck, 1962.

3 M. Delvoye points out that the presence of the 'Fleurs de Lys' and the 'confronted lions' of the Lusignans suggest that the church was founded by Manuel Cantacuzenos (1348-80) whose wife was Isabella de Lusignan 'Chronique archéologique' in *Byzantion*, XXXIV, 1964, p. 160. Also see his 'Mistra', in *Corsi di Cultura*, 1964, p. 127.

4 The date of 1428 for the rebuilding is accepted by Chatzidakis, *Mistra*, p. 85, but disputed by D. Zaky-

thinos, *Despotat Grec du Morée*, II, pp. 286 and 298. The paintings must, however, belong to around that year.

5 K. D. Kalokouri, *The Byzantine Wall Paintings of Crete*, Athens, 1957 (in Greek).

6 M. Chatzidakis, *Icones du Saint Georges des Grecs et de la Collection de l'Institut Hellénique de Venise*, Venice, 1962, no. 50, plates VI and 37. It was shown at the Byzantine Exhibition at Athens in 1964, no. 272.

7 These monasteries have never been very fully published. The most complete series of plates will be found in V. R. Petković, *La Peinture Serbe du Moyen âge*, Belgrade, 1930. See also S. Radojćić, *Les Maîtres de l'Ancien Peinture Serbe*, Belgrade, 1955.

8 M. Chatzidakis, 'Theotokopoulos and Cretan Painting' from *Kritika Chronica*, Heraklion, 1950, discusses the question of Greco's Cretan heritage and concludes that his Spanish style owes more to the colouristic art of Venice and to the mannerism of Rome than to his Greek origin. Greco may have begun as an icon painter, but arrived in Venice, it was the new elements with which he came into contact that really affected his work. But he does owe to Crete his realization of the value of deformation of natural forms to achieve a given aim, the precision and clarity of his compositions, his economy of space and the importance laid on the human figures which contrasts markedly with the complexity of composition and subordination of the figures in

Tintoretto's work. Others have laid greater stress on his Byzantine origins; for the most recent survey of this aspect see L. Hadermann-Misguich, 'Forme et esprit de Byzance dans l'œuvre du Greco', in *Revue de l'Université de Bruxelles*, No. 5, Aug.-Sept., 1964.

9 *The Byzantine achievement*, London, 1929, p. 220. See also *The Birth of Western Painting*, p. 7.

10 The question of Greco's Byzantine affinities was first raised by Don Pedro de Madrazzo as early as 1830; they were noted by Cossio in 1906, Sir Charles Holmes in 1924 and Meier-Graefe in 1927, and were examined in closer detail by Robert Byron, first in an article in the *Burlington Magazine*, LV, 1929, p. 160 f., entitled 'Greco: The Epilogue to Byzantine Culture', and then in collaboration with the writer, in *The Birth of Western Painting*, 1930; see p. 8 for a survey of writings on the subject up to then. Theories as to Greco's early life in Crete were first proposed by Mr. A. A. Xyrou in a book in modern Greek published in 1932 and entitled *Domenikos Theotokopoulos, the Cretan;* they were summarized in English by Mr Frank Rutter in the *Burlington*, Vol. LX, 1932, p. 274, under the title 'The Early Life of el Greco'. In 1930 P. Schweinfurth devoted a study to the subject 'Greco und die Italo-Cretische Schule', *Byzantinische Zeitschrift*, XXX, and in 1937 by R. Palluchino, in his *Il Politico del Greco della R. Galleria Estense*, Rome, 1937. Greco's Byzantinism was further discussed briefly by the writer in the *Burlington*, Vol. LXX, 1937, p. 34, under the title 'El Greco and Byzantium'. More recently the problem has been reconsidered in a general way by Pál Kelemen, *El Greco Revisited*, New York, and in the more specialized study of the subject by Miss Hadermann-Misguich, already cited.

11 For the former see Byzantine Exhibition Catalogue, no. 271. Lord Crawford's icon was included in the Byzantine exhibition held at Edinburgh and in London in 1958; see *Masterpieces of Byzantine Art*, Edinburgh-London, 1958, no. 202.

12 For the most recent examination of the debt to engravings; see L. Hadermann-Misguich, 'Deux nouvelles sources d'inspiration du triptique de Modena' in *Gazette des Beaux Arts*, Mai-Juin, 1960 p. 355; see also: Hadermann-Misguich, 'Forme et Esprit de Byzance dans l'œuvre du Greco', in *Revue de l'Université de Bruxelles*, 5 Août-Sept., 1964, p. 5; see also L. A. Meyer, 'Notes on the early El Greco', in the *Burlington Magazine*, LXXIV, 1939, p. 28.

13 Robert Byron, 'Greco: the Epilogue to Byzantine Culture', in the *Burlington Magazine*, LV, 1929, p. 171 and plate 127.

14 A. Muñoz, *I Quadri Bizantini della Pinacoteca Vaticana*, Collezione Archeologiche, X, Roma, 1928, no. 37, plate XIX, no. 2.

15 H. E. Wethey, *El Greco and his School*, Princeton, 1962, I, p. 31 and II, p. 198

16 L. Bréhier, *L'Art Chrétien: son dévelopment iconographique*, Paris, 1928, p. 136.

Index

Figures in italic type refer to the black and white plates, those in Roman numerals to the colour plates.